The Son of Man

Zacchaeus Studies: New Testament

General Editor: Mary Ann Getty

The Son of Man

A Metaphor for Jesus in the Fourth Gospel

Mary Margaret Pazdan, O.P.

A Michael Glazier Book
THE LITURGICAL PRESS
Collegeville, Minnesota

A Michael Glazier Book published by The Liturgical Press.

Scriptural quotations are from the Revised Standard Version unless other-wise noted.

1	2	3	4	5	6	7	8	9

Library of Congress Cataloging-in-Publication Data

Pazdan, Mary Margaret, 1942–
    The Son of man : a metaphor for Jesus in the Fourth Gospel / by Mary Margaret Pazdan.
       p.   cm. — (Zacchaeus studies. New Testament)
    "A Michael Glazier book."
    Includes bibliographical references.
    ISBN 0-8146-5677-3
    1. Bible. N.T. John—Criticism, interpretation, etc. 2. Son of Man. 3. Jesus Christ—Person and offices—Biblical teaching. I. Title. II. Series.
BS2615.6.S57P38   1991
226.5'064—dc20   91-26977
                                                              CIP

Contents

Editor's Note

Zacchaeus Studies provide concise, readable and relatively inexpensive scholarly studies on particular aspects of scripture and theology. The New Testament section of the series presents studies dealing with focal or debated questions; and the volumes focus on specific texts or particular themes of current interest in biblical interpretation. Specialists have their professional journals and other forums where they discuss matters of mutual concern, exchange ideas and further contemporary trends of research; and some of their work on contemporary biblical research is now made accessible for students and others in *Zacchaeus Studies*.

The authors in this series share their own scholarship in nontechnical language, in the areas of their expertise and interest. These writers stand with the best in current biblical scholarship in the English-speaking world. Since most of them are teachers, they are accustomed to presenting difficult material in comprehensible form without compromising a high level of critical judgment and analysis.

The works of this series are ecumenical in content and purpose and cross credal boundaries. They are designed to augment formal and informal biblical study and discussion. Hopefully they will also serve as texts to enhance and supplement seminary, university and college classes. The series will also aid Bible study groups, adult education and parish religious education classes to develop intelligent, versatile and challenging programs for those they serve.

Mary Ann Getty
New Testament Editor

Introduction

When will the world end? What will happen when it does? How will believers be united with God? In the middle of the first century, Paul found these questions challenging as he formed his first community of believers. In writing to the community at Thessalonica, Paul included a description of the second coming of Jesus whose descent from heaven would initiate the resurrection of believers into the clouds to meet the Lord (1 Thess 4:16-17). This description which is interpreted literally by some Christian communities today is called the "rapture."[1] Throughout Christian history, too, imaginations and hearts nourished by biblical stories, preaching, art, music, and poetry keep alive the apocalyptic hopes about the end time. The same questions which challenged Paul continue to have their impact on contemporary communities.

The expectation of Jesus' second coming may recall for many Christians the Gospel which is proclaimed for the First Sunday of Advent. To inaugurate a new liturgical year for the community, the Church uses Christ's vivid description of the end time and his exhortation to vigilance:

> And there will be signs in sun and moon and stars, and upon the earth distress of nations in perplexity at the roaring of the sea and the waves, men fainting with fear and with foreboding of what is coming on the world; for the powers of the heavens will be shaken. And then they will see the Son of man coming in a cloud with power and great glory. Now when these things

[1] E. Whisenant, *On Borrowed Time: 88 Reasons Why the Rapture Will Happen in 1988* (Nashville: World Bible Society, 1988).

9

begin to take place, look up and raise your heads, because your redemption is drawing near. . . . "But take heed to yourselves lest your hearts be weighed down with dissipation and drunkenness and cares of this life, and that day come upon you suddenly like a snare; for it will come upon all who dwell upon the face of the whole earth. But watch at all times, praying that you may have strength to escape all these things that will take place, and to stand before the Son of man." (Reading for Year C: Luke 21:25-28, 34-36.)

The image of the Son of man as an apocalyptic judge in this Advent reading was continued and developed in Christian tradition. How Jesus is related to the eschatological judge as well as to other descriptions of the Son of man in the Gospels is an important consideration in contemporary New Testament studies. The fact that Son of man sayings occur in the Four Gospels only where they are attributed to Jesus emphasizes the particular character of both the interest and the puzzle.[2]

New Testament scholars have been engaged in vigorous discussions about the Son of man since the challenge in 1965 to earlier scholarship. Lively debates about the origin, meaning, and interpretation of the term and concept have continued in journals, monographs, and conferences where Synoptic scholars concerned with the Gospels of Matthew, Mark, and Luke constitute the predominant group. Their different methods and interests are apparent when they address the issues. Studies based on Semitic philology, in particular, have challenged earlier scholarship about the function of the Son of man as a Christological title.

In contrast, the Son of man sayings in the Fourth Gospel have not often been discussed in their relationship to the Synoptic traditions. In their pursuit of other areas of investigation, Johannine scholars are seldom involved in discussion of the Son of man verses within the Gospel.

Another focus of the Son of man investigation is its relationship to Christology. While the identification may have been an

---

[2]Four verses in the New Testament are indirect references to Jesus as Son of man: John 12:34, a comment by the crowd; Acts 7:56, a speech of Stephen; Revelation 1:13; 14:14, a visionary description which cites Daniel 7:13.

important insight for *early* believers in the Risen Jesus in the Gospels, the terminology did not appear significant in Pauline or other early Christian literature nor in the definitive Christological councils of Nicaea and Chalcedon. Nonetheless, new interest about Son of man formulations is emerging today in the dialogue between biblical scholars and systematic theologians considering how recent biblical scholarship may have an impact on the foundations of New Testament Christologies.

In the last decade, pastoral sensitivity to the issue of inclusive language encouraged a rethinking of the term "Son of man" for worshiping communities. In a newly revised translation of the New Testament, while "Son of man" is retained, annotation of the verses indicates current scholarship that includes the designation "a human being."[3] The formal equivalent of "Son of man" is translated "Human One" in the *Inclusive-Language Lectionary* since the committee believed the same nuances of interpretation are common to both terms.[4]

In this book, Son of man identifies an area of contemporary research as well as biblical and non-biblical references. The capitalization of "Son" and *not* "man" gives the reader an opportunity to decide whether the evidence for the titular function, Son of Man, or a non-titular function, son of man, is convincing. The Revised Standard Version (RSV) and Common Lectionary use Son of man in their respective translations.

My primary interest in the current investigation is to explore the function and significance of Son of man *within* the Fourth Gospel as a contribution to Johannine Christology as well as a *dialectic* for the Synoptic contours of the discussion. This focus of interest on the Fourth Gospel is developed in three parts:

Part One provides a context for understanding the Fourth Gospel by presenting a limited historical survey of some aspects of Synoptic and Johannine studies. A review of Synoptic studies gives attention to the status of the apocalyptic Son of man and

[3]See Mark 8:31 par in *The Revised New Testament of The New American Bible* (New York: Catholic Book Publishing, 1986).

[4]Inclusive-Language Lectionary Committee (National Council of Churches), *An Inclusive-Language Lectionary: Readings for Year C* (Atlanta: Knox; New York: Pilgrim; Philadelphia: Westminster, 1985) 259–60.

evaluates the scholarship. A review of Johannine studies focuses on the origin and function of the Son of man sayings and an evaluation of the scholarship. Part One concludes with a description of the method which constitutes the interpretive framework for Part Two.

Part Two is an analysis of the Fourth Gospel according to the story genre. Narratives and discourses which illustrate the function of the Son of man in the story of Jesus are discussed. The structure of the examination corresponds to the major divisions of the Gospel: Prologue (1:1-18); Book of Signs (1:19-12:50); Book of Glory (13:1-20:31). The Epilogue (21:1-25) is not considered in the analysis.

Part Three examines the relationship of the analysis of the Fourth Gospel (Part Two) to New Testament Christologies. Contemporary perspectives on methods in Christology are outlined. The question of a Christology of the Johannine Son of man is addressed. The author's interpretation is presented.

Part One:
The Son of Man in Synoptic and Johannine Scholarship

This section presents a selected survey of scholarship on the origin, meaning, and function of the Son of man as a term and concept in the Four Gospels. A distinct change of focus for Synoptic studies occurred in 1965. Up to that time, most scholars had assumed that a firm foundation existed in apocalyptic literature for the presence of a transcendent, messianic figure as the origin for Son of man in the Synoptic Gospels. Beginning in 1965, scholars challenged that assumption and radically shifted the course of scholarly inquiry and debate.

In contrast, Johannine studies about the Son of man have not created as much controversy or been such a challenge as the Synoptic studies. The distinctiveness of the gospel genre as well as its high Christology appeared to preclude numerous studies. As interest in the origin of the Son of man sayings waned, the function of the sayings as a Christological focus increased. Correspondingly, the relationship between stages of Gospel composition/community and Christological statements provided a basis for a new focus on the Son of man sayings.

1. The Focus of the Synoptic Gospels

a. Challenge of New Testament Semitists

Before 1965, the Son of man discussion centered on two questions: (1) the origin and meaning of the term and concept; (2) the authenticity and interpretation of the sayings in the Synoptic Gospels. The conclusions about the second question influenced the direction of the first question. Most scholars had accepted the analysis of Rudolf Bultmann who classified the sayings into three categories: "(1) as coming, (2) as suffering death and rising again, and (3) as now at work." Authentic sayings were limited to the first group which designated an eschatological judge (Mark 8:38, 13:26, 14:62; Luke 11:30; 12:8f. par., 17:24 par., 17:26f. par.). The sayings, however, did not constitute a self-identification for Jesus.[5] Other scholars held minority positions by identifying all three categories or none of the categories as authentic sayings. The first question, then, became a search for a significant locus for the term and concept. H. E. Tödt is representative of those scholars who established an integral connection between the description of the future Son of man in Jewish apocalyptic literature (Dan 7:13f., 4 Ezra, Similitudes of Enoch) and the Son of man in the Synoptic Gospels.[5a] They located in the apocalyptic literature a concept of a transcendent, messianic figure who would exercise final judgment over all persons at the end of time.

By 1965, however, New Testament Semitists challenged the earlier scholarship.[6] They insisted that any exegetical understanding of the Son of man in the Gospels ought to begin from a solid linguistic base. Researchers investigated the origin of Son of man which appears in the Gospels in two Greek forms. One form, *ho huios tou anthrōpou*, is found only in the Jesus sayings in the Synoptics and the Fourth Gospel. It is not a Greek idiom since both nouns "son" *(huios)* and "man" *(anthrōpou)* have definite articles *(ho, tou)*. The formation called "arthrous" (with articles) may be translated "the man's son" or "the son of the man." The

---

[5]R. Bultmann, *Theology of the New Testament* (2 vols; New York: Scribner's, 1951-1955) 1. 29-31.

[5a]H. E. Tödt, *The Son of Man in the Synoptic Tradition* (trans. D. M. Barton; London: SCM, 1965).

[6]For articles which review the Son of man scholarship, see John Bowker, "The Son of Man" *JTS* 28 (1977) 19-48; William O. Walker, "The Son of Man: Some Recent Developments" *CBQ* 45 (1983) 584-608; John R. Donahue, "Recent Studies on the Origin of 'Son of Man' in the Gospels" (Festschrift for J. A. Fitzmyer) *CBQ* 48 (1986) 484-98; Adela Yarbro Collins, "The Origin of the Designation of Jesus as 'Son of Man' " *HTR* 80 (1987) 391-408.

other form, *huios anthrōpou* called "anarthrous" (without articles) is translated "son of man." It occurs less frequently in the New Testament and is interpreted as a translation of a Hebrew construction, i.e., a Semitism.

Where did the unusual arthrous construction *ho huios tou anthrōpou* originate? Semitic linguists investigated Greek, Hebrew, and Aramaic literature. A survey of non-Christian Greek literature before the New Testament offered no evidence while a survey of the Hebrew Bible and the Mishnah for arthrous and anarthrous *ben'adām* constructions yielded meager results. Aramaic literature, however, held more promise. It became the *primary* area of investigation.

Scholars had discussed the functions of Son of man in Palestinian Aramaic *(bar nāsh/bar nāsh[ā])* since 1896. Most of them agreed that the phrase was commonly used as a generic noun ("a person," "the person") and as an indefinite pronoun ("someone," "anyone"). Two disputed uses were as a circumlocution for the speaker ("I") and as a title whose use Synoptic scholarship had taken for granted.

b. Vermes-Fitzmyer Debate

In 1965, Geza Vermes presented his discoveries on the function of *bar nāsh/bar nāsh(ā)* in Jewish Aramaic.[7] Working with Rabbinic sources, he offered evidence for the circumlocutional use of the phrase in the Palestinian-Galilean idiom of the second century C.E. Moreover, nothing in his study had convinced Vermes that the Aramaic phrase had been used as a *title* in a messianic context. The crucial text of Daniel 7:13f. was mitigated to "one like a son of man." Vermes challenged New Testament exegetes with a dilemma: *Either* the Greek arthrous construction is derived from the Aramaic phrase whose usage does not include titular significance *or* it is an unusual, original phrase accepted by the evangelists but neglected later by the Church.

For a decade, Vermes' position evoked sharp debate principally with Joseph A. Fitzmyer. From his own study, Fitzmyer concurred

---

[7]Vermes delivered a paper at Oxford to the International Congress of Biblical Studies. The printed version appeared in his "Appendix E: The Use of *Bar Nash/Bar Nasha*" in M. Black, *An Aramaic Approach to the Gospels and Acts* (3d ed.; Oxford: Clarendon, 1967) 310–28.

with Vermes about the generic and indefinite use of the Aramaic construction as well as the lack of examples for titular designation, especially to identify an apocalyptic, messianic figure. However, its use as a circumlocution to identify the speaker ("I") was another matter.[8] Fitzmyer argued that Vermes' sources (e.g., Palestinian Talmud, targums, midrashim) were dated later than the Aramaic material prior to the New Testament. In addition, those texts represented later Aramaic constructions which could not be used as evidence for first-century Palestinian usage.

Vermes, in turn, referred to later Aramaic constructions present in first-century Galilean contexts. He maintained that when Jesus used "son of man" he employed it in situations of awe, reserve, or humility as a circumlocution. Vermes' proposal limiting the phrase exclusively to Jesus' reference to himself ("I and no other") stimulated new discussion.

Another proposed source for the apocalyptic Son of man had been 1 Enoch. When the textual fragments of Qumran were published, however, the material essential to the argument, namely, the Similitudes of Enoch, chapters 37–71, were not found. Since an argument from silence is not definitive, the ensuing dispute over the dating of the Similitudes had to be resolved before the text could be employed in the Son of man dispute. Several scholars suggested a period between the middle of the first century B.C.E. and the end of the first century C.E. thereby submitting the Similitudes as an appropriate source for the titular use of *bar nāshā*. Others argue that the witness of a reconstructed text would be slight. There is no consensus about the significance of the text.

c. Norman Perrin and Literary Criticism

At the same time as New Testament Semitists questioned an apocalyptic Son of man, Norman Perrin, a pioneer in the method of literary criticism, also challenged earlier scholarship. From his analysis of Jewish apocalyptic writings (Dan 7; 1 Enoch; 4 Ezra),

---

[8]For publications which indicate the nature of the discussion, see: G. Vermes, *Jesus the Jew* (London: Collins, 1973) 160–91 and "The 'Son of Man' Debate" *JSNT* 1 (1978) 19–32; J . A. Fitzmyer, "Another View of the 'Son of Man' Debate" *JSNT* 4 (1979) 58–68; "The New Testament Title 'Son of Man' Philologically Considered" in *A Wandering Aramean: Collected Aramaic Essays* (*SBLMS* 25; Missoula: Scholars, 1979) 143–60 and *The Gospel According to Luke I-IX* (*AB* 28; Garden City: Doubleday, 1979) 208–11.

he concurred about the absence of both an eschatological Son of man title and concept in Jewish thought. He also denied the authenticity of *all* Son of man sayings attributed to Jesus. Perrin proposed that the sayings were the creation of early Christian communities reflecting on the Hebrew Scriptures in light of Jesus' resurrection. Using Daniel 7:13 as a basic text, three exegetical traditions developed: a future coming (Mark 13:26); an ascension which interpreted the resurrection in light of Psalm 110:1 (Mark 14:62a); and a passion statement employing Zechariah 12:10ff. (John 19:37; Matt 24:30). Perrin determined that the process which early communities used to interpret the Hebrew Scriptures was similar to the exegetical pattern at Qumran. There, the *pesher* method of the community was based on an exegesis of its writings in light of the community's experience of living at the end time of history.

d. Daniel 7:13-14 and the Son of man Sayings

A decade later, three scholars applied the Semitic data to investigate the relationship of Daniel 7:13-14 to the Synoptic Son of man sayings. From Aramaic sources, Maurice Casey found that the Son of man phrase functioned as a generic noun in statements where a speaker would declare something about himself which would often include a group of associates. The speaker used the construction to avoid "sounding exceptionally exalted or feeling exceptionally humiliated."[9] In applying the generic idiom to Daniel 7, there was no evidence for a Son of man *concept*. Casey identified the figure "one like a son of man" in Daniel 7:13 as a *symbol* of the vindicated Jews who had suffered under Greek domination. He rejected the interpretation of a corporate figure (i.e., the suffering community of Israel called to be faithful to God) as well as the personalization of that figure in the self-understanding of Jesus (i.e., the suffering one who would be vindicated by God). In applying the generic idiom to the Synoptic sayings, Casey refuted Vermes' claim that Jesus used the term exclusively to refer to himself. Jesus used the phrase without any *special* designation. The statements were generic observations

---

[9]M. Casey, *Son of Man: The Interpretation and Influence of Daniel 7* (London: SPCK, 1980) and his " 'Son of Man'—General, Generic and Indefinite" *JSNT* 29 (1987) 21–56.

about himself and others; for example, Mark 2:10 indicates a general notion of healers who forgive sins.

An analysis of New Testament texts attributed to Daniel 7:13 convinced Casey that its influence was minimal for the early Church and non-existent for Jesus. Using the generic idiom, he reconstructed a core of authentic *present* Son of man sayings, i.e., statements which indicate the *earthly activity* of Jesus (Matt 12:32//Luke 12:10; Matt 8:20//Luke 9:58). Conversely, sayings which used *ho huios tou anthrōpou* but did not correspond to the Aramaic phrase were not authentic. The *passion* sayings, i.e., statements which indicate the *suffering* of Jesus, originated from a generic statement about the inevitability of death, a concept found in the Old Testament, for example, in Genesis 2:17 and Isaiah 40:6-8. Jesus predicted his fate with a general statement about death and resurrection. The expanded sayings in the Gospel reflect the traditions which arose in the early Church after his death and resurrection. *Future* sayings, i.e., statements about Jesus' *second coming*, developed as a midrash on Daniel 7:13. When the Gospel traditions were written down, the Aramaic idiom was translated by the arthrous Greek phrase. The *definite articles* indicate that the generic nature of the sayings had been lost; consequently, the sayings became an exclusive description of Jesus.

A. J. B. Higgins represents another perspective which itself indicates development.[10] In 1964, Higgins maintained that the origin of the Son of man concept existed in Jewish apocalyptic literature. By 1980, he located the distinctiveness of the idea in the Gospels. He agreed that the Aramaic phrase as an indefinite pronoun ("anyone") could be the basis for some authentic "present" sayings: for example, Mark 2:10 and Matthew 8:11. Nonetheless, most authentic sayings are located in the *kernel* statements of Q (Luke 11:29ff., 12:8f., 17:22, 24, 26f., 28-30). In these future sayings, Jesus' use of the Son of man emerges to indicate the role which he would assume after his death when God would vindicate him. He would be exalted and given the role of the eschatological judge described in Jewish apocalyptic literature. The distinctiveness of Jesus' use of the Son of man concept was in

---

[10]A. J. B. Higgins, *The Son of Man in the Teaching of Jesus (SNTSMS* 39; Cambridge: University, 1980). Cf. his *Jesus and the Son of Man* (London: Lutterworth, 1964).

applying his ideas about judgment, for example, "the sign of Jonah," in symbolic language.

Building on the study of Aramaic sources by Vermes and Casey, Barnabas Lindars proposed another definition of the Son of man: an oblique self-reference ("a person in my position").[11] In Aramaic texts, he located an idiom (one with a generic article) for those situations when a speaker refers to a class of persons with whom there is identity. Applying this idiom to the Gospels, Lindars isolated nine authentic sayings of Jesus where the Aramaic *bar (e)nāsh(ā)* was the basis for the Greek translation *ho huios tou anthrōpou*. The *article* is present in both constructions. The authentic present and passion statements indicate a non-titular use of Son of man with no allusion to Daniel 7:13. In contrast, a chief characteristic of the unauthentic, future sayings is the use of Son of man as an exclusive self-reference in which the allusion to Daniel 7:13-14 is explicit.

e. Evaluation

The debate about the origin and meaning of Son of man as a term and concept appears deadlocked. New Testament Semitists insist on a thorough investigation of the Aramaic background as a prelude for approaching the Synoptic Gospels. There is agreement only about the lack of evidence in Jewish sources for an apocalyptic, messianic Son of man with titular significance. Scholars variously attribute a generic, indefinite, exclusive, or oblique, self-reference to Aramaic Son of man passages. There is on-going discussion about grammar as well as the dating, selection, and use of particular texts the lack of which may hinder the study.[12]

---

[11]B. Lindars, *Jesus Son of Man* (Grand Rapids: Eerdmans, 1983).

[12]For evaluations of various positions, see I. H. Marshall, "The Son of Man in Contemporary Debate" *EvQ* 42 (1970) 67-80; F. J. Moloney, "The End of the Son of Man?" *DowR* 98 (1980) 280-90; C. Tuckett, "Recent Work on the Son of Man" *ScrB* 12 (1981-1982) 14-18. For debate issues, see C. Tuckett, "The Present Son of Man" *JSNT* 14 (1982) 58-81; M. Black, "Aramaic Barnasha and the 'Son of Man' " *ExpT* 95 (1, 1984) 200-5 and M. Casey, "Aramaic Idiom and Son of Man Sayings" *ExpT* (8, 1985) 233-36; C. Mearns, "The Son of Man Trajectory and Eschatological Development" *ExpT* 97 (1, 1985) 8-12; R. Bauckham, "The Son of Man: 'A Man in my Position' or 'Someone'?" *JSNT* 23 (1985) 23-33 and B. Lindars, "Response to Richard Bauckham: The Idiomatic Use of Bar Enasha" *JSNT* 23 (1985) 35-41; W. Horbury, "The Messianic Associations of 'The Son of Man' " *JTS* 36 (1985) 34-55.

The variety of linguistic conclusions provides a broad range of possible ways in which the Son of man idiom may have been used in first-century C.E. speech patterns. When the judgments were applied to the Synoptic Gospels, they addressed two basic questions: Whom did the idiom identify? Was *additional* meaning intended? Linguistic data and presuppositions influenced the process which resulted in a diversity of opinions about the authenticity and interpretation of the Synoptic sayings.

The contributions of New Testament Semitists to Synoptic exegesis can be examined within the framework of the new search for the historical Jesus. First, several clusters of criteria are applied to a text to locate the original words of Jesus.[13] One criterion is determining the Palestinian context of a pericope. If a Greek passage indicates a Semitism, i.e., *ho huios tou anthrōpou/bar (e)nāsh(ā)*, it is evidence for an Aramaic original attributed to Jesus. While Jesus probably spoke Galilean Aramaic, three other languages were characteristic of first century Palestine—Greek, Latin, and Hebrew. Given the cultural conditions of Palestine, Jesus may have been bilingual. A Semitism may also identify either Palestinian Christians who developed a gospel tradition or a writer composing in Greek whose first language is Aramaic. The catalyst for the translation of the Aramaic phrase into the strange "arthrous" Greek construction has not been identified. The ambiguities involved in establishing a Palestinian context limit a clear decision. The criterion is considered secondary to dissimilarity, coherence, and multiple attestation. The nuanced application of a Palestinian context, however, provides a response to two methodological considerations which were not explicit in the Semitic research: (1) How and when may Aramaic sources be used to illumine a Synoptic text? (2) On the other hand, to what extent ought the Synoptic sayings *per se* be used as evidence for a Jewish background?

Second, the categories to designate Jesus' teaching vary and influence its status. Some scholars retain the Bultmann classification of three types of Son of man sayings while others chal-

---

[13]For a survey and evaluation of the new search for the historical Jesus, see D. Polkow, "Method and Criteria for Historical Jesus Research" *SBL Seminar Papers* 26 (Atlanta: Scholars, 1987) 336–56.

lenge it. Vermes' analysis had been based on the relationship of the sayings to Daniel 7:13-14 while Tödt and others approached them according to form and function. The attributed use of the Aramaic Son of man in the Gospels determined the authenticity of the sayings. The denial of a Jewish, apocalyptic Son of man from Semitic sources resulted in identifying the future sayings as the provenance of Christian communities.

Third, New Testament study of the Gospels is moving from a focus on establishing the original words of Jesus to interpreting what they mean. This current direction is a corrective to the tendency to isolate the reconstruction of the original words of Jesus from the literary features and Christological perspectives of an entire Gospel. The exegetical method of New Testament Semitists, too, tended to study the Son of man sayings in Mark in isolation from the structures of the Gospel. Similarly, conclusions about Marcan sayings were applied to Matthean and Lukan verses with the same results.

Fourth, scholarly interpretations of Jesus' teaching, which are increasing in number and variety of emphasis, rely less on one (i.e., Aramaic background) or many criteria for determining Jesus' original words. Historical, literary, and sociological methods are employed for selected passages in the context of what a particular Gospel describes about Jesus' life, death, and resurrection. What emerges is a diverse picture of the historical Jesus which affirms the multiple Christologies in the New Testament.[14]

2. The Focus of the Fourth Gospel

a. Distinctiveness of the Gospel

A survey of selected Synoptic literature on the Son of man indicates that the testimony of the Fourth Gospel had been virtually discounted. Methodologically, it is difficult to situate the Son of man sayings in the Fourth Gospel within the categories represented in the relatively uniform sayings of the Synoptic Gospels. The predominance of realized eschatology in the Fourth Gospel substan-

---

[14]For a review of approaches for the historical Jesus, see Irvin W. Batdorf, "Interpreting Jesus since Bultmann: Selected Paradigms and Their Hermeneutic Matrix" *SBL Seminar Papers* 23 (Chico: Scholars, 1984) 187–215.

tially negates the future sayings and renders them as present sayings: for example, God gave Jesus the authority to judge because he is the Son of man (5:27), a heavenly being who came into the world. In addition, Jesus' suffering which is a component of his "hour" is intimately connected with a return to that "glory" which he had before the creation of the world. The assumption that the Fourth Gospel reflected later developments of Synoptic traditions limited its value for understanding the origin and concept of the Son of man. In particular, the presence of a high Christology and extensive redaction activity of earlier traditions restricted its witness.

b. Dissertations

The reduced status of the Son of man sayings in the Fourth Gospel in Synoptic studies is expressed within Johannine literature itself. Fewer Johannine than Synoptic scholars were involved in Son of man investigations. Two dissertations are included in the extant literature. In 1953, Siegfried Schulz traced the development of the Son of man concept through a combination of the history of religions and tradition criticism.[15] His new method investigated how historical-cultural factors might influence a passage. He examined several types of passages which he classified according to a *theme*—Son of man, Son, Paraclete, and Second Coming. Each theme is a traditional unit derived from the Jewish Apocalyptic figure in Enoch. Each theme had been reinterpreted by different groups (Hellenistic Gnostics, Jews, and Jewish Christians) before it was employed in the composition of the Fourth Gospel. Son of man sayings are either directly dependent on the apocalyptic Son of man (1:51; 3:13-15; 5:27-29; 6:27, 53; 13:31-32) or less dependent with the addition of "ascending/descending" and "lifting up/glorification" (6:62; 8:28; 12:3-34). Schulz also classified a few of the sayings according to their literary genre: midrash (e.g., 1:51; 3:13-15; 5:27-29); homily (6:27, 53); and hymn (13:31-32).

In 1975, Francis J. Moloney investigated the meaning of Johannine Son of man in a theological context.[16] He reviewed and

[15]S. Schulz, *Untersuchungen zur Menschensohn-Christologie im Johannesevangelium* (Göttingen: Vandenhoeck und Ruprecht, 1957).

[16]Francis J. Moloney, *The Johannine Son of Man* (2nd ed.; Rome: LAS, 1978) 1-22; see also a summary of his dissertation in "The Johannine Son of Man" *BTB* 6 (1976) 177-89.

evaluated the status of opinions about a Johannine Son of man Christology before examining each Son of man saying in its wider context—for example, types of faith (John 2:1–4:54)—as well as in its particular context—for example, narrative. He concluded with specific distinctions about the function of Son of God and Son of man in the Fourth Gospel. The first term, "Son of God," was used to describe Jesus' relationship with the Father before, during, and after his incarnation while the second term, "Son of man," was limited to Jesus' ministry. As Son of man, Jesus revealed God with supreme authority because of his unique relationship to the Father. Judgment occurs when an individual believes or refuses to believe in Jesus' testimony in which the cross is a supreme moment of revelation.

In the appendix written for the second edition, Moloney discussed how the Son of man was related to the developing Christology of the Johannine community. He suggested three functions of the Johannine Son of man: (1) to correct Jesus' identification as the traditional Jewish Messiah; (2) to insist on Jesus' revelation of God especially at the cross; and (3) to use *language* indicative of late first-century syncretism whose *content* did not contain earlier Christian tradition. The community although principally Jewish was in conflict with the synagogue as it developed a particular understanding of Jesus as the Son of man. The title which drew attention to Jesus' humanity may have been a foil for any misunderstanding of the Son of God Christology.[17]

c. Origin of the Son of man Sayings

The perspectives about the origin and function of the Son of man considered in the dissertations appear in other studies of the past three decades. Commentators on the Gospel proposed sources and influences for the Son of man sayings which corroborated Schulz' research. C. H. Dodd located the idiom in the archetypal or ideal person of Hellenistic literature[18] while C. K. Barrett identified the archetypal figure in the heavenly man of Jewish

[17]Moloney, App. to Diss., 221–56, esp. 254–55.

[18]C. H. Dodd, *The Interpretation of the Fourth Gospel* (Cambridge: University, 1953, rpt. 1970) 241–49.

apocalyptic (Dan 7:14; 4 Ezra; 1 Enoch).[19] For Wolfgang Roth, the Abel narratives and Genesis 1-11 may be the background.[20] Similarly, Jewish exegetical traditions—for example, Sinai—offer possibilities according to Peder Borgen.[21] Others proposed some relationship of the Johannine sayings with the Synoptic sayings. S. S. Smalley suggested that the Johannine sayings might be earlier than the Synoptic sayings due to their kerygmatic preciseness,[22] while Frederick Borsch determined that the Son of man sayings were "more primitive" than other Johannine logia.[23] For Robert Maddox there was a continuity of the Fourth Gospel with the Synoptics.[24] When Jesus is acting on his own initiative, he judges and imparts life as the Son of man. Rudolf Schnackenburg, too, identified some use of Synoptic traditions in the Johannine text.[25] While the suffering and future activities of the Son of man are similar, however, he surmised that there had been a thorough development and transformation of the traditions to correspond to the Christological perspective of the Fourth Gospel.

d. Function of the Son of man Sayings

Another important consideration of the Son of man sayings is how they function in the Gospel. Here, too, different methodological viewpoints are evident. A few scholars considered the role secondary. Edwin Freed applied the *variety* characteristic of the literary style of the Gospel to its use of proper names and titles

[19]C. K. Barrett, *The Gospel According to St. John* (2nd ed.; Philadelphia: Westminster, 1978) 61 and *passim.*

[20]W. Roth, "Jesus as the Son of Man: The Scriptural Identity of a Johannine Image" *The Living Text: Essays in Honour of Ernest W. Saunders* (eds. D. W. Groh and R. Jewett; New York: University of America, 1985) 11-26.

[21]P. Borgen, "Some Jewish Exegetical Traditions as Background for Son of Man Sayings in John's Gospel (3, 13-14 and context)" *L'Evangile de Jean: Sources, rédaction, theologie (BETL* 44; ed. M. de Jonge; Leuven: University, 1977) 254-58.

[22]S. S. Smalley, "The Johannine Son of Man Sayings" *NTS* 15 (1968--69) 278-301, esp. 299.

[23]F. Borsch, *The Son of Man in Myth and History* (Philadelphia: Westminster, 1967) 257-313.

[24]R. Maddox "The Function of the Son of Man in the Gospel of John" *Reconciliation and Hope: New Testament Essays on Atonement and Eschatology* (Festschrift for L. L. Morris; ed. R. Banks; Grand Rapids: Eerdmans, 1974) 186-204.

[25]R. Schnackenburg "Excursus V: The 'Son of Man' in the Fourth Gospel" *The Gospel According to St. John,* 1 (Montreal: Palm, 1968) 529-42.

for Jesus.[26] The qualities and activities of the Son of man are also attributed to the Son, Son of God, and "I am" *(egō eimi)* sayings. Maurice Casey, who denied the influence of Daniel 7 on the Synoptic sayings, extends this judgment to the Fourth Gospel as well. Although his discussion is limited to John 1:51 and 5:27, Casey concludes that the Son of man is one of several alternative descriptions which the author could use to describe Jesus.[27] Similarly, J. Massingberd Ford identified a relationship between Son of man and Son of God based on the Jewish notion of euphemism especially in reference to a divine name.[28] She specified several verses which link the Son of man and a divine attribute. For example, Nathanael addresses Jesus as Son of God (1:49), but Jesus responds in a Son of man saying (1:51).

Others suggested an integral function. Highlighting the spiral development of the Gospel, Elisabeth Kinniburgh interpreted the Son of man sayings within the context of sayings about Father/Son and "I am" *(egō eimi)*.[29] She concluded that together the sayings reveal the whole story of Jesus (present, suffering, future activities) as realized eschatology.

e. Son of man Sayings and Stages of Gospel Composition/Community

In addition to Moloney, several interpreters have linked the function of the sayings with a particular stage of their composition within the Johannine community.[30] From his theory of two editions, Barnabas Lindars located most of the Son of man sayings in the first edition which drew on earlier traditions about

---

[26]E. Freed, "The Son of Man in the Fourth Gospel" *JBL* 86 (1967) 402–09.

[27]M. Casey, *Son of Man*, 197–99.

[28]J. M. Ford, "The 'Son of Man'—A Euphemism?" *JBL* 87 (1968) 257–66.

[29]E. Kinniburgh, "The Johannine 'Son of Man' " in *Studia Evangelica*, 4 (ed. F. Cross; Berlin: Akademie, 1968) 64–71.

[30]The designation "community" identifies a group of persons for whom the Johannine understanding of Jesus and a life patterned according to the perception are essential. Occasionally, the plural form is used to describe persons who left the early group due to disagreements about what constitutes the community. See R. E. Brown, *The Community of the Beloved Disciple* (New York: Paulist, 1979).

Jesus.[31] The Evangelist reinterpreted the passion prediction as the source for the other sayings using Daniel 7, and its development in Jewish apocalyptic to express Jesus' relationship to God. In John 3:14 Jesus becomes God's agent of revelation. Through his ministry, the Johannine Jesus offers proleptically to believers what will be at the end time—life through death.

From another literary theory of the Gospel as a two-level drama, J. Louis Martyn also attributed an integral function to the Son of man.[32] In the first stage (Jesus of Nazareth), believing included identifying Jesus as the Mosaic messiah because of his signs (miracles). The midrashic expansions in the Gospel indicate that this identification could be discussed (e.g., 3:2 and 4; 6:14 and 30ff.). In the second stage (the Johannine community in conflict with a synagogue), identifying Jesus as the Son of man represents a more adequate stage of believing. The absence of the midrash precluded any discussion of this concept (e.g., 9:35ff.). The Johannine Son of man encapsulates past, present, and future time in his activities of descending, judging, and ascending.

Koyoshi Tsuchido recognized the conflictive situation of the community with the synagogue as the historical circumstance from which high Christology developed.[33] Using tradition and redaction criticism in his analysis of John 11:55–12:43, he proposes how the Evangelist's activity of linking 12:32 and 34 leads the community to his understanding of the pre-existent glorified Christ within the earthly life of Jesus as the Son of man.

Jerome H. Neyrey examined Son of man verses within their immediate contexts to determine the level of Christological development.[34] His analysis of some verses indicated a juxtaposition of a Synoptic saying about the suffering Son of man (low Christology) with a Johannine saying about pre-existence or glorification (high Christology): 3:13-14; 5:27; 6:62; 8:28; 1:51.

---

[31]B. Lindars, "The Son of Man in the Johannine Christology" *Christ and Spirit in the New Testament* (Festschrift for C. F. D. Moule; eds. B. Lindars and S. S. Smalley; Cambridge: University, 1973) 43–60 and his *Jesus Son of Man*, 145–57.

[32]J. L. Martyn, *History and Theology in the Fourth Gospel* (rev.; Nashville: Abingdon, 1979) 120–42.

[33]K. Tsuchido, "Tradition and Redaction in John 12.1-43" *NTS* 30 (1984) 609–19.

[34]J. Neyrey, "The Jacob Allusions in John 1:51" *CBQ* 44 (1982) 586–604.

For Wayne Meeks, the descending/ascending Son of man is a literary/theological motif which defines the social setting of a community that understood itself as unique and alienated from its world because of its belief in Jesus.[35] The language is descriptive of a changed social status which includes symbolic language to verify its existence.

In contrast, Margaret Pamment denied that the Son of man is a Christological term.[36] It does not function to distinguish Jesus' unique characteristics. Using the contributions of New Testament Semitists about the generic use of the Son of man, Pamment argued that the sayings indicate a specific intention. Each is explicable in light of Daniel 7:13 to indicate "Jesus' representative humanity" which offers possibilities for human life. In the Son of man statements, Jesus is described as the one who understands heavenly things and reveals God's life in his death. He acts as God does in giving life and exercising judgment. Accordingly, those who believe in him will share his humanity, i.e., his life, glorification, and exercise of judgment.

f. Evaluation

Background influences to which scholars have attributed the Son of man sayings in the Fourth Gospel included Jewish sources and exegetical practices, Aramaic speech patterns, and relationships to Synoptic traditions. While interest in the sources waned, the foci on the function of the sayings became more extensive. Schulz' early work in 1953 may have been a prophetic statement about current scholarship. His proposal about the influence of different groups upon themes (including the Son of man sayings) is found in contemporary studies involved in the relationship of Christological terms derived from perceptions of members of the Johannine community.

If the Son of man sayings have a more integral function than an alternative description of Jesus, what is it? According to Moloney, it is a corrective to Son of God Christology. Each title indicates distinctive qualities of Jesus. Other scholars, however, would also compare Son of man with Son and "I am" *(egō eimi)*

---

[35]Wayne Meeks, "The Man from Heaven in Johannine Sectarianism" *JBL* 91 (1972) 44–72.

[36]M. Pamment, "The Son of Man in the Fourth Gospel," *JTS* 36 (1985) 56–66.

to designate a particular stage of development. What situation of the community called for the Son of man sayings? How did the situation influence the function of the sayings in the Gospel?

In the literature about sources and function of the sayings, the methodological procedure is similar. The *modus operandi* is an examination of certain verses to ascertain a particular viewpoint. The tendency to atomize the text into discreet units of probable provenance, Christological insight, authentic Jesus tradition, and parallels to the Synoptic sayings may narrow and dim the horizons of the Gospel.

g. *Another Method and Rational*

An overview of the Gospel as story, however, provides a different perspective. With one exception (13:31), the Son of man sayings occur in the Book of Signs (1:19–12:50). Its structure combining a mixture of characters who interact in narratives invites the reader to consider the possibility of believing in Jesus. That the invitation is an inclusive one is indicated by the deliberate choice of persons, named and unnamed, who encounter him. The terms by which Jesus is identified either by himself or others represent the mixture of settings, plots, and characters. None of the terms appear to be in competition with one another. There is no *explicit* preference for a particular identification among the disciples, the crowds, the Pharisees, or Jesus. Occasionally, terms occur in parallel structure—"I am" *(egō eimi)* and Son of man (6:51-53)—or in close proximity to one another—Son of man and Son (3:13-17). The terms, like the well-developed narratives and discourses of the Book of Signs, function to invite belief in Jesus.

The structure of the Book of Glory (13:1–20:31) which indicates a similar mixture of narratives and discourses (with the latter predominating) is a challenge addressed to a more limited readership—those who already believe in Jesus. The Son of man saying in 13:31 describes how Jesus' hour will be accomplished. It is inserted into a sequence of action and discourse where Jesus' example and teaching as well as his interaction with his disciples reveal his identity linked with those who follow him. Irony and double-layered meanings for words and actions which were operative in the Book of Signs are evident here as well.

An analysis of a few identifying terms for Jesus proceeding from a historical-critical perspective does not constitute Johannine Christology. Beginning with the post-resurrection situation of the Johannine community, reconstructing a probable context for development does not exhaust the function of the Son of man or other Christological categories. In these approaches, the text is secondary to the presuppositions of the interpreter.

What may expand the investigation is to recall the fluid development of the scenes, their episodic nature, and the unexpected shift of dialogues into monologues intermeshed with repetitions, details, and an implicit summons toward the symbolic possibilities of the text. Interpreting the Gospel as a literary text whose story form is inseparable from its content is an alternative method. It offers the possibility of more than one function for Christological terms and their relationship to the Johannine story of Jesus which is not limited to one group of readers. In particular, the metaphorical use of terms for Jesus may be a response to the tension over his identity indicated in the encounter of Jesus with various characters.

Part Two: The Son of Man in the Fourth Gospel

This section is an interpretation of the identity of Jesus as it is disclosed through the narrator and characters of the Gospel. The method used considers the story form of the text inseparable from its content. The reader is invited to consider the names which the narrator and various characters give to Jesus as well as those he uses for himself within the broader horizon of character and plot development. Particular Johannine literary devices (e.g., misunderstanding, irony, double meanings) are noted to highlight the symbolic possibilities of the text. The interpretation follows the major divisions of the Gospel: Prologue (1:1-18); Book of Signs (1:19–12:50); Book of Glory (13:1–20:31).

1. The Prologue (1:1-18)

The narrator startles the reader with the very first phrase of the Prologue: "In the beginning" (v. 1). *Whose* beginning? Cosmic, human, personal? Concomitant with the indeterminate time "was the Word and the Word was with God, and the Word was God" (v. 1). Invited to participate in that opaque period *before* time began, the reader ponders: How is God in relationship with the Word? How is the Word both "with God" and "God"? Suddenly drawn *into* time, the reader listens as the Word creates the cosmos and endows human beings with life, with that true *(alēthenon)* light which no darkness can destroy (vv. 2-4, 9).[37] How

---

[37]"True" *(alēthinos)* is a Johannine adjective used nine times to designate what is "genuine" and "real."

can the cosmos and his very own family reject the light? Some believe in his name. Begotten by God, they are empowered to be God's children (vv. 10-13). Surely, God would do no more.

Readers are scarcely able to catch a breath after the proclamation when their attention is riveted on the *next* verse: "And the Word became flesh and made his dwelling among us" (v. 14a NAB). How can the Word *(Logos)* whose presence began before time enter into human history at its most basic and intimate level? Imagination grasping for insight wrestles with the collective witness of believers: "and we saw his glory, the glory as of the only begotten *(monogenēs)* of the Father, full of grace and truth. . . . No one has ever seen God. The only begotten *(monogenēs)* God, who is in the bosom of the Father, that one has revealed him" (vv. 14b, 18 NAB).

The Prologue functions as a clear and unambiguous testimony revealing outside and within time who Jesus is and how he is related to God and creation. As the pre-existent *Logos*, the only begotten Son *(monogenēs)* of the Father, Jesus became the incarnate, unique communication of God.

Given the confessional quality of the Prologue, some scholars have wondered why the Gospel as story genre is necessary. As story, the Gospel invites participation both with the characters and the plot. The intricate interweaving of symbols, irony, and misunderstanding within the development of characters and plot enables the reader, regardless of a *specific* identity, to become an integral part of the drama. The involved reader can determine whether or not the witness of the Gospel confirms the testimony of the Prologue. Experience is essential for making the decision about whether to believe or not to believe in Jesus as the pre-existent *Logos* and the incarnate Son of God and Son of man.

Literally and theologically, the Prologue functions as the center panel in a triptych. In this position, it draws attention to itself as well as to its relationship to the other two parts of the Gospel. On the left side is the Book of Signs (1:19–12:50) where Jesus invites persons to believe in what he says and does. On the right side is the Book of Glory (13:1–20:31) where Jesus describes what being in relationship means since it includes more than relationship with Jesus.

2. The Book of Signs (1:19–12:50)

a. The Baptizer's Witness and the First Disciples

The continuity of the Baptizer's function in the Prologue (1:6-8, 15) and in the opening scene of the Gospel (1:19-34) is one indication of the *spiral* technique used in the Gospel. Its strategy of introducing an idea at one point in the narrative and then developing that same idea at another point assists the reader to collapse the time differential with a renewed sense of past and present episodes. As witness to the light, the Baptizer was clearly distinguished from the light (1:6-8, 15). As the first-named voice in the Gospel, he refutes any claims to being either the Messiah, Elijah, or one of the prophets.[38] In his subordinate, preparatory role, he baptizes and points out Jesus' identity to his disciples. Heralding Jesus as the Lamb of God, the one upon whom the Spirit descends and dwells, the Baptizer testifies that Jesus is the Son of God (1:19-34). His testimony draws two of his disciples to Jesus.

They, in turn, bring others to Jesus (1:35-51). Each new invitation to see Jesus is marked with another disclosure of his identity: Rabbi (vv. 38, 49), Messiah (v. 41), him of whom Moses in the law and also the prophets wrote (v. 45), Son of God (v. 49), King of Israel (v. 49). Jesus neither affirms nor denies any identification. The rapid succession of titles is an escalating expression of beliefs ranging from human acceptance—for example, Rabbi—to divine origin and designation—Son of God and King of Israel. All titles appear eclipsed by Jesus' enigmatic statement: "Truly, truly, I say *(amēn, amēn legō)* to you, you will see heaven opened, and the angels of God ascending and descending upon the Son of man" (v. 51 NAB).[39] The metaphor which frames this

---

[38]RSV consistently translates *Christos* as "Messiah" throughout the Fourth Gospel while NAB transliterates *Christos* as "Christ." *Messia,* which is the Greek transliteration of the Aramaic word, occurs only two times in the Gospel on the lips of the disciples Andrew (1:41) and the Samaritan woman (4:25). The narrator interprets the unusual *Messia* noun for the readers as *Christos* (1:41c; 4:25 b). The judgment of RSV is better since it acknowledges the Jewish background of the term. The NAB translation of "Christ" may suggest to some readers that the noun is a Christological title which is anachronistic. The author follows the RSV rendering.

[39]The "truly, truly, I say" *(amēn, amēn legō)* expression is a Johannine formula used twenty-five times to begin a solemn declaration by Jesus. Its first appearance here to introduce a

title, Jesus' first disclosure of himself as the Son of man, presents a new insight drawn from earlier titles. The incarnate *Logos* is the one whose being is the divine presence as well as the access to God.

b. Nicodemus

In contrast to this gradual illumination about Jesus, Nicodemus, a Pharisee who comes to him at night, remains in twilight. Given the symbolic dark/light dichotomy which identifies the cosmos/Jesus (1:10-11), Nicodemus initially represents a group who does not accept Jesus. A comparison of the Baptizer and the early disciples with Nicodemus reveals striking differences in their positions. First, geographical indicators express dissimilarity. The Baptizer and the early disciples, although called in Judea, were from Galilee, a region whose population was considered less religiously observant than persons who lived in Judea, especially near Jerusalem. Nathanael, whom Philip seeks out, expresses a typical Judean's dismissal of the Galilean region when Philip identifies Nazareth as Jesus' home: "Can anything good come out of Nazareth?" (1:45-46). Nicodemus is a Judean. Second, unlike the Baptizer and the disciples, he embodies the fullness of religious authority: a Pharisee, a member of the Jewish Sanhedrin, (one who holds) the office of teacher of Israel (3:1, 10). Third, without spending time with Jesus as the early disciples did (1:39), Nicodemus takes the initiative with Jesus by recognizing *his* credentials at their first meeting: Rabbi, one come from God, a worker of signs, one to whom God is present (3:2).

With Nicodemus' credentials and an assessment of Jesus introduced in the first two verses, the entire scene is crafted to unfold Nicodemus' symbolic characterization. Jesus' response, which does not comment on Nicodemus' identification, begins the dialogue. Jesus declares the necessity of being "born from above" in order to "see the kingdom of God" (v. 3). Nicodemus misunderstands the metaphor. As a literalist, he conjures up the image of an old man returning to his mother's womb. The play

---

Son of man saying expresses the importance of the teaching. The same pattern appears in 6:53. Other uses of the formula also introduce Son of man sayings. See 5:19, 24, 25 for v. 27; 6:26 for v. 27; 12:24 for v. 34; 6:21 for v. 31.

on the phrase "from above"/"again" *(anōthen)* did not occur to him (v. 4). Jesus develops his statement by equating "water" and "Spirit" with "born from above" (vv. 5-8). When Nicodemus protects his reputation and tradition by asking how it will happen, Jesus is surprised that he does not understand (vv. 9-10). Monologue abruptly replaces dialogue. The speakers "I" and "we" (Jesus and the community of believers) insist that the testimony is based on knowing and seeing. How can Nicodemus accept "heavenly things" if he does not believe "earthly things"? (vv. 11-12). The rhetorical question ironically functions to alert the reader to a response based on the ability to perceive "heavenly things."

The monologue clarifies Jesus' enigmatic statements (vv. 5-8) by describing *how* an individual is "born of the Spirit":

> No one has gone up to heaven except the one who has come down from heaven, the Son of Man. And just as Moses lifted up the serpent in the desert, so must the Son of Man be lifted up, so that everyone who believes in him may have eternal life (vv. 13-14 NAB).

The narrator integrates several transformations of the tradition. The ascending-descending activity of the angels of God (1:51) is identified with the Son of man. The time frame of future expectation about a Son of man is collapsed to identify one who has already come down from heaven and will return (v. 13a). Using a well-known, life-giving symbol associated with Moses' activity during the Exodus, the narrator indicates how the Son of man will return to heaven: by being lifted up (v. 14). The spatial language is inherently related to the Johannine chronology of Jesus' "hour" as his suffering, death, and resurrection. The "lifting up" *(hupsōthēnai)* of the Son of man refers specifically to his crucifixion and return to the Father, acts which give eternal life to believers (vv. 14-15).

The explanation of how the Son of man is related to the Prologue occurs in the next section of the monologue (vv. 16-21). God's love for the cosmos is so extraordinary that God sends the only Son *(monogenēs)* to give believers eternal life, not death (v. 16). The Son is not sent to condemn but to save the cosmos (v.

17). The one who believes will not be condemned. However, the one who does not believe in the name of the only Son *(monogenēs)* of God is already condemned (v. 18). What is the condemnation? The one who does not believe has preferred darkness to the light. The one who engages in evil activities hates the light for it exposes evil works (vv. 19-20). Those who believe, however, live the truth *(alētheian)* and act openly, showing that their activities are clearly rooted in God (v. 21).[40]

No longer will the Son of man judge each person at the end time. To the contrary, belief in the Son of God is the decisive judgment which directs a life rooted in God, in the light. For the one who does not believe, there is self-condemnation and a life rooted in evil and in darkness. The coming together of a freely chosen decision to believe or not to believe with a type of self-judgment determines the individual's present and future direction. The decision, while not conclusive is expressed in daily life with activity congruent to it.

The identity of the speaker in verses 31-36 is unclear. While the teaching is variously attributed to Jesus, the Baptizer, and the narrator, the intention is to comment on the function of the Son. The descending Son of man (v. 13) is described as the one "who comes from above *(anōthen)* . . . who comes from heaven" (v. 31). He alone is the one "whom God has sent" to "witness to what he has seen and heard" (vv. 32, 34). The Father who loves the Son has given everything to him (v. 35). The one who believes in the Son has eternal life. Conversely, the one who does not obey the Son will not see life (v. 36). Here the uniqueness of the Son consists in his witness to what he has heard God say and do. Those who believe in his words enter into life. Accepting his testimony is another dimension of believing in him. Notice how the additional descriptions for the Son (from above, from heaven, witness, sent, loved) complement those of the Prologue and delineate the activities of the Son of man (1:10-14, 18).

How Nicodemus responded to the monologue is not indicated, but when he appears a second time, the Pharisees are discussing

---

[40]"Truth" *(alētheia)* is a favorite Johannine term used twenty times to indicate the dichotomy between it and statements and activities forged in darkness and lies. See 1:14, 17; *3:21*; 4:23, 24; 8:32, 40, 44, 45, 46.

the possibility of arresting Jesus. Nicodemus asks them if it would be proper procedure since Jewish law doesn't condemn a person "without first giving him a hearing and learning what he does (7:50-51). The Pharisees taunt him: "Are you from Galilee, too?" (7:52a). Since he speaks up, Nicodemus' status suffers. In his final appearance, he assists Joseph of Arimathea with Jesus' burial. He brings "a mixture of myrrh and aloes about a hundred pounds' weight" (19:38-42).

The portrayal of Nicodemus is consistent. The phrase which introduces him, "came to him" (3:2), is repeated in other appearances (7:50; 19:39). Although it may describe only his physical approach to Jesus, the phrase probably suggests Nicodemus' initial readiness to believe in him. His silence in response to Jesus' monologue (3:11-21) is also repeated when the Pharisees taunt him (7:52). His concerns about legal precision and explusion from the group appear to be greater than his courage to witness on Jesus' behalf. Again, Nicodemus does not speak up with Joseph of Arimathea to secure Jesus' body from the authorities. He is silent while he helps prepare Jesus' body for burial. A clue to his behavior is his association with Joseph, "a disciple of Jesus, but secretly, for fear of the Jews" (19:38).

c. *The Samaritan Woman*

Jesus' encounter with the Samaritan woman at the well (4:4-26, 39-42) provides an opportunity for the reader to savor the irony involved in the characterization of various disciples in the Fourth Gospel. The woman functions as a perfect foil for Nicodemus. Contrasts in both setting and religious/social status emphasize the woman's marginal position: In Sychar (v. 5) at noon (v. 6), an unnamed "woman of Samaria" comes to draw water (v. 7). Functioning as a *teacher*, she reminds Jesus of both the hostile relationship between Jews and Samaritans (v. 9) and the tradition about the well (vv. 11-12).

Unlike the structure of the Nicodemus story where dialogue turns into monologue, lively dialogue is the primary vehicle for Jesus and the woman. Misunderstanding is the key to recognizing how the metaphor "water" can be interpreted on two levels. Physically, there is the need for water (vv. 11-15). Spiritually, Jesus alone provides "living water" (vv. 16-26). Within this dialogue, the woman reveals her deepening insights about Jesus wherein his identity as "you, a Jew" (v. 7) and "Sir" (vv. 11, 15) are inadequate. She then addresses him as "prophet" (v. 19) and "Messiah" (v. 29; cf. 1:41, 45). She, like Nicodemus, addresses others. However, she acknowledges her encounter with Jesus to the townspeople. Drawn by her proclamation, they, in turn, seek out Jesus asking him to spend time with them. In the final scene, one hears the insight of the townspeople: "We know that this is truly *(alēthōs)* the Savior of the world" (vv. 39-42).[41]

The woman's status, marginal when compared with Judeans, Galileans, and even her own townspeople, is completely reversed by her deep commitment as a disciple of Jesus. She represents Jesus' invitation to every person regardless of background. In contrast, Nicodemus, whose status in Jerusalem was assured, lacked the imagination and courage to reconsider traditional viewpoints. His colleagues respected him, yet fear prevented him from answering their rejoinder.

The story of the woman of Samaria follows the pattern of the two disciples of the Baptizer who were led to Jesus because of John's word. After spending time with Jesus, the two disciples shared their experience and brought others to him (1:35-45). The Samaritan woman is both unlike the Judeans in the Temple who demanded a sign from Jesus (2:18-22) and similar to the Galilean official who believed in Jesus' word before seeing the confirming sign (4:46-54). Her courage in speaking the truth about her own experience separates her from Nicodemus as well as from the paralytic by the pool whose fear led him to a different response.

d. The Paralytic

When Jesus takes the initiative to heal the paralytic, conflict arises (5:1-16). The paralytic is condemned by the Jews for carrying his mat on the Sabbath (v. 10). While he had not even known Jesus' name when he was cured, afterwards he reports Jesus to the authorities. Did he wish to mitigate his own condemnation by supplying Jesus' name as a wonder worker (v. 15)? He freed

---

[41]"Truly" *(alēthōs)* is a Johannine adverb used seven times to express the genuineness of a declaration. See also 1:48; 6:14.

himself from any conflict of choice which a relationship to Jesus might entail. In contrast, the Pharisees' conflict with Jesus led to their persecuting him "because he did this [healing] on the Sabbath" (v. 16).

The controversy over healing on the Sabbath becomes an occasion for Jesus' teaching (5:17-46). The triple occurrence of the "truly, truly, I say" *(amēn, amēn, legō*; vv. 19, 24, 25) formula indicates the solemnity of the instruction. It is *not* a dialogue. On the contrary, Jesus responds to the Jews who seek to "kill him because he not only broke the Sabbath but also called God his own Father, making himself equal to God" (v. 18). The intimate relationship predicated by the Father-Son language is scandalous. That Jesus as the beloved Son is dependent upon the Father to do what he sees his Father doing, including raising the dead and giving them life, adds to the implicit charges of blasphemy (vv. 19-21).

A third activity, judgment, is also predicated of God. The Father authorizes the Son to judge precisely "because he is the Son of man" (vv. 22-23, *27).* Eschatological judgment, however, is now. Eternal life is hearing Jesus' word—hearing the voice of the Son of God—and believing in the one who sent him (vv. 24-25). Paradoxically, while the Father has given all judgment to the Son, the latter cannot judge on his own authority: "as I hear, I judge; and my judgment is just, because I seek not my own will but the will of him who sent me" (v. 30). Everything which Jesus hears and sees in the Father's presence, "in the bosom of the Father" (1:18), constitutes what he reveals about the Father through his word and works. This comprehensive revelation of the Father can be accomplished solely through the only Son *(monogenēs)* of God who is also identified as the Son of man.

The sign *(sēmeion)* followed by discourse is a literary pattern common to chapters five and six. Variety is established through different settings, *dramatis personae* (characters), plot, and climax. The geographical designations of either Galilee or Judea for earlier characters established an ironic polarity where the Judeans became foil characters. Their inadequate or total failure to believe in Jesus (see 2:18-23; 3:11-12) is in strong contrast to the disposition of the Galileans who firmly believed in him (1:45-46; 4:46-54). In chapter six, the geography shifts from Jerusalem to the "other side of the Sea of Galilee" or the "other side of the sea" (vv. 1, 25). The *dramatis personae* of chapter five (Jesus, a paralytic, the Jews) are replaced and enlarged by a "multitude" (vv. 2, 5), "disciples" (v. 3, 22, 24, 60, 61, 66), "Philip" (vv. 5, 7), "Andrew" (v. 8), "people" (vv. 14, 22, 24), and "Jews" (vv. 41, 52). Jesus identified as Son and Son of man in chapter five retains these designations as well as new ones (Lord, Rabbi, bread of life, son of Joseph, Holy One of God).

The plot's development in chapter five from healing to confrontation with the Jews continues in chapter six. Both healing and feeding are life-giving activities of Jesus who continues his Father's works. The hostility of the Jews toward Jesus' claims continues in the dialogues between Jesus and the crowds and with the disciples. The climax in each narrative is based on acceptance or rejection of Jesus. What distinguishes the narrative of chapter six from the previous chapter's is the dynamic development within the feeding narrative and dialogues as well as in their sequential connection.

e. The Feeding Sign and Discourse

In the feeding pericope (vv. 1-14), the disciples are distinct from the multitude. Their activities include sitting with Jesus (v. 3), being involved with the problem of feeding the multitude wherein Philip and Andrew are prominent (vv. 7-9), giving directions to the crowd (v. 10), and gathering up the fragments (vv. 13-14). The activities of the multitude are juxtaposed with those of the disciples in order to reveal the stages of becoming a disciple. The inclusion technique (vv. 2, 14) indicates that the multitude responded to Jesus' signs. They followed him because they had seen his signs (v. 2). The people proclaimed their understanding of his identity after they were fed: "This is truly *(alēthōs)* the prophet who is to come into the world!" (v. 14 NAB). The signs were catalysts for drawing them to Jesus. The multitude "coming to him" (v. 5) also suggests some type of readiness to believe in Jesus. Nonetheless, they follow Jesus because they are seeking a generous wonder-worker. Their enthusiastic proclamation, accompanied by the plan to take him by force to make him a king, is thwarted by Jesus' departure (v. 15). Perhaps their belief in him needs development. The portrait of the named and unnamed disciples provides a contrast to the healed paralytic who seeks no relationship with Jesus.

The dialogical structure of the discourse material begins when the people question Jesus about his new location (v. 25). Jesus' response evaluates their insufficient grasp of him: "Truly, truly, I say *(amēn, amēn legō)* to you, you seek me, not because you saw signs, but because you ate your fill of the loaves" (v. 26). He challenges them to work for "food" which will never perish, which the Son of man will provide (v. 27). The parallel to "living water" (4:13-14) is subtle. The escalating movement from being fed on the hillside (v. 11) and seeking the bread giver (v. 26) to asking about how to do God's work (v. 28) is rapid. Jesus assures them that doing God's work is believing in the one whom God has sent (v. 29). Seeking further assurance, they ask him what sign he will offer them to authenticate himself as someone greater than Moses who pleaded with God for bread in the desert. The narrator implies that the crowd does not remember the feeding (vv. 30-31). Jesus asserts, "truly, truly, I say" *(amēn, amēn legō)* that it is not Moses but only the Father who can give the true *(alēthinon)* bread from heaven which gives life to the world. "Lord, give us this bread always" (vv. 32-34). Both the woman at the well (4:15) and the crowd accept Jesus' gift of life which remains forever. At this point in the respective dialogues, there is no recognition of the gift. For the people in the present dialogue, Jesus is Rabbi and Lord. Jesus identifies himself as the Son of man on whom God the Father has set his seal (v. 27).

The climactic statement of revelation occurs in the center of the dialogues while the remaining verses clarify and extend the declaration. Jesus identifies himself as the bread of life which satisfies all hunger and thirst for the one who believes in him (v. 35). Immediately, the people who are certain that he is "Jesus, the son of Joseph," dispute this identification. How can Jesus be the one "come down from heaven" (v. 42)? How can his flesh be "the bread for the life of the world" (v. 51)? The questions and murmuring focus on the impossibility of Jesus giving his flesh to eat (v. 52). Jesus insists: "Truly, truly, I say" *(amēn, amēn legō)* there is no life for any one person unless that one person eats the "flesh of the Son of man and drink(s) his blood." The eating and drinking are essential for eternal life. They are true *(alēthēs)* food and drink for the believer who already experiences mutual abiding with Jesus (vv. 53-56).[42] Throughout the dialogue, Jesus consistently refers to his dependency upon the Father for his life, giving life, and judging (vv. 37-40, 44, 57).

While the people engage Jesus in conversation, the disciples are silent. There is no indication that the people turned away from Jesus. It is the disciples who assume the earlier postures of the people when they murmur about whether they can accept Jesus' disclosure (v. 61). Jesus challenges them to imagine even more: "Then what if you were to see the Son of man ascending where he was before?" (v. 62). It is a proleptic announcement of Jesus' *hour* as the Son of man. Many disciples could no longer follow Jesus. Peter confirms him as the Holy One of God, an oblique description which does not capture the clarity of the Son of man (v. 69).

f. The Feast of Tabernacles

The intention of persecuting Jesus because of his claims and his activities on the Sabbath (ch. 5) continues in Jerusalem during the feast of Tabernacles (7:1-44). The ominous note already introduced in the confrontation of Jesus with the authorities who "sought all the more to kill him" (5:18) resounds several times (7:19, 20, 25, 30, 44-45). For many of the people in the crowd, Jesus' teaching raises the possibility of his being the Messiah (vv. 26, 31). Nevertheless, the Jerusalemites, like the people whom Jesus fed, are certain they know his origin while the origin of the Messiah is unknown (v. 27; 6:42-43; cf. 1:41; 4:29). Their certainty echoes ironically in Jesus' response: "You know me, and also where I come from" (v. 28 NAB). It is an opportunity to speak of his relationship to the Father: "He who sent me is true *(alēthinos)*, and him you do not know. I know him, for I come from him, and he sent me" (vv. 28-29).

The sudden approach of the officers sent by the Pharisees and chief priests signals Jesus' declaration about his impending hour (v. 32). Only "a little longer" *(chronon mikron)* separates Jesus from his departure to the one who sent him. The search to find

---

[42]"True" *(alēthēs)* is another Johannine adjective used nine times to indicate "genuine" or "real"; cf. n. 37.

him will be ineffective because "where I am you cannot come" (vv. 33-34). Misunderstanding his statement, the Jews suppose he may be going to teach the Greeks (v. 35). The repetition of Jesus' statement as a puzzling one for the Jews underscores its importance (v. 36). The reader perceives multiple ironies underlying the impossibility of the Jews to be with Jesus no matter how they search for him. In addition, their supposition that Jesus will teach the Greeks is a proleptic comment about the Greeks' seeking Jesus later (12:20ff.). The debate reaches a climax when the narrator comments: "There was a division *(schisma)* among the people over him" (v. 43).

The symbol of light associated with Tabernacles is the link to the next dialogue which Jesus initiates with the Jews. "I am the light of the world. Whoever follows me will not walk in darkness, but will have the light of life" (8:12 NAB). The statement suggests a spiral movement wherein the unquenchable light introduced in the Prologue as the life for all persons (1:4-5) is now identified as Jesus. His pronouncement here parallels the prose comment in the Prologue: "The true *(alēthinos)* light, which enlightens everyone, was coming into the world" (1:9 NAB). The adjective "true" qualifies "bread" (6:32) and "light" (8:12) in order to designate Jesus as the embodiment of these primary symbols of life.

The Pharisees object to Jesus' statement saying it cannot be true *(alēthēs)* since Jewish law demands that personal testimony be confirmed by another witness (v. 13). Jesus asserts that his testimony and judgment are true *(alēthēs/alēthinē)* since the Father testifies on his behalf (vv. 14a, 16-18). Jesus alone knows his origin and destination. "You know neither me nor my Father; if you knew me, you would know my Father also" (vv. 14b, 19b; cf. 7:28).

Jesus initiates a dialogue with the Pharisees which repeats his earlier statements to the Jerusalemites where he announces his imminent departure and their inability to follow him (v. 21; cf. 7:33-34). Two variations in the statements are important. First, the declaration "you will not find me" (7:34a) becomes "you will die in your sin" (8:21b). The inability of the Pharisees to "find" Jesus in the sense of coming to him for life (believing in him) is equated with dying in sin. Second, the clause "where I am"

(7:34b) becomes "where I am going" (8:21b) followed by "you cannot come" in both verses. The statement suggests that Jesus dwells in a place which is inaccessible to the Jews—that is, always with the Father. The Jews cannot "find" Jesus nor share in his dwelling because they believe neither in him nor in the Father. Furthermore, they cannot participate in Jesus' solitary journey through his hour now, nor will they share in it later.

The Pharisees, like the Jerusalemites, misunderstand Jesus. They wonder if he is going to kill himself (v. 22; cf. 7:35). Their misunderstanding is typical of Johannine characters who interpret Jesus' sayings on a physical level—for example, Nicodemus and the Samaritan woman. Jesus, however, provides enlightenment with additional teaching which is consistently on a spiritual level. In this context, Jesus points out the two different spheres in which the Pharisees and he live. They will "die in their sin" being "from below" and "of this world" while Jesus is "from above" and "not of this world" (v. 23). Only believing in Jesus will give them life and a new realm of existence. "For if you do not believe that I AM, you will die in your sins" (v. 24 NAB). While "I am" *(egō eimi)* may be interpreted literally, the meaning is Christological in the Fourth Gospel. Whether it appears as pronoun and verb ("I am") or as pronoun, verb, and noun ("I am the living bread"), the phrase reminds the reader of the divine name revealed to Moses on Mount Sinai (Exod 3:14).

What sign will Jesus offer to prove that his testimony is true? "When you lift up the Son of Man, then you will realize that I AM, and that I do nothing on my own, but I say only what the Father has taught me" (v. 28 NAB). Just as Jesus challenged Nicodemus, the Pharisee, with the need for the Son of man to be lifted up (3:14), now Jesus challenges other Pharisees to believe that the Son of man is "I am" in that same event. The reader recognizes a double irony. Jesus challenges the Pharisees to participate in the "lifting up" which is another proleptic note referring to Jesus' hour. The concern of the Pharisees to prove the truth of Jesus' testimony is reversed in the telling comment of the narrator: "As he spoke thus, many believed in him" (v. 31). The final use of "I am" in 8:58, however, results in the Jews' rejection of Jesus: "They took up stones to throw at him" (v. 59). The overarching tension apparent in the narrative (chs. 5–8) is whether to accept Jesus' testimony about himself. The tension is resolved by denial (8:59).

g. *The Man Born Blind*

The placement of the narrative about the man born blind (ch. 9) immediately following the chapters concerning denial turns the reader's world upside down. While Jerusalem is the common setting, the characters and dialogues appeal persuasively for acceptance of Jesus. The disciples begin the narrative with a question about whose sin is responsible for the man's blindness (vv. 1-2). Jesus, however, indicating that the man is a visible manifestation of God's works, immediately identifies himself with that work by proclaiming: "I am *(egō eimi)* the light of the world" (v. 5b; cf. 8:12). Mixing the earth with his saliva, Jesus applies it to the man's eyes and directs him to go to the pool of Siloam. The man obeys and comes back with his sight restored (vv. 6-7).

Confusion about identity characterizes the dialogues in chapter nine. It is easy to imagine neighbors kibitzing over the fences about the blind man's identity (vv. 8-9). Talk surely continued after the man born blind declared his identity and told how Jesus' anointing gave him sight for the first time in his life (vv. 9b-11). In responding to his neighbor's question, the man was unclear only about Jesus' whereabouts (v. 12).

The scene shifts abruptly to the Pharisees' interrogation of the man healed on the Sabbath (vv. 13-15). Unlike the neighbors who listened to his story, the Pharisees argued among themselves about whether or not Jesus was a sinner; it caused a division *(schisma)* among them. The blind man, however, was certain: "He is a prophet" (vv. 16-17, cf. 1:45). Not satisfied, the Pharisees summoned the man's parents in order to hear their testimony. Frightened, his parents told the Jews: "Ask him; he is of age, he will speak for himself" (vv. 18-23).

Still dissatisfied, the Pharisees again summon the man born blind to repeat his story, but they now concur that Jesus is a sinner. Unwilling to repeat it, the man born blind questions their ability to listen. "Do you too want to become his disciples?" (vv. 24-27). Exasperated, the Pharisees tell him that they are Moses' disciples whereas "you are his disciple." After all, it is a question of knowing origins. We know about Moses, but Jesus? (vv.

28-29). The man born blind teaches the Pharisees: "Unless this man were from God, he could do nothing" (vv. 30-33). Judging the young man to be steeped in sin, they throw him out of the synagogue (v. 34).

The purpose of the narrative is revealed in the fifth dialogue which is between Jesus and the man born blind. Jesus reveals himself explicitly when he asks, "Do you believe in the Son of man?" (v. 35; cf. 1:50). It is the apogee of the blind man's identifications (vv. 11, 17, 33). The man asks for clarification (v. 36). When Jesus confirms that he is the Son of man, the man's experience with various confrontations centered about Jesus comes to a climax, and he responds: "Lord, I believe" (v. 38).

In the last episode, the Pharisees listen to Jesus teaching the man born blind about judgment and the paradox of seeing yet being blind. While the narrator does not explicitly introduce them as witnessing to the blind man's confession, nonetheless, they are present afterwards. Intending to exonerate themselves, they instead condemn themselves: "Are we also blind?" (vv. 39-40). Jesus verifies their self-judgment: "Your guilt remains" (v. 41). The confusion over Jesus' identity is resolved. The blind man sees and follows the light whereas the Pharisees remain in the dark, blinded by their disbelief. Jesus' declaration about "dying in your sin" (8:21) "unless you believe I AM" (8:24) is acted out in the Pharisees who refuse to believe in Jesus as the Son of man.

The geographical indicators in chapters six through nine reach a new conclusion. While various Galilean characters continue to believe in Jesus (ch. 6), the Judean characters reject him (chs. 7-8). The man born blind is the only Judean character who believes in Jesus. Ironically, his healing and his subsequent belief in Jesus influence the Pharisees of Jerusalem to reject him.

Jesus' activity continues in Judea (chs. 10–12) where the growing hostility against him is in marked contrast to a few who believe in him. When Jesus identifies himself with "I am" *(egō eimi)* and calls himself "the door of the sheep" (10:7, 9), "the good shepherd" (vv. 11, 14), the Jews fail to understand. Jesus' declaration that the Father loves him because he freely lays down his life is a source of division *(schisma;* vv. 17, 19). Characteristically unsure if he is the Messiah, the Jews ask Jesus to speak plainly (v. 24). Jesus repeats that the works he has done in the

Father's name confirm his testimony. He gives eternal life to those whom the Father has given him (vv. 25-29). Jesus' proclamations about his identity are familiar to Judean crowds. His new declaration: "I and the Father are one" (v. 30) is met with their charges of "blasphemy because you, being a man, make yourself God" (v. 33). The narrator records three retaliations against Jesus: two attempted stonings and an arrest (vv. 31, 33, 39) as well as a note about the many people who believed in Jesus because of the Baptizer's testimony (vv. 41-42).

h. The Raising of Lazarus

The literary pattern of sign *(sēmeion)* and discourse common to the previous narratives (chs. 5, 6, and 9) is reversed in the raising of Lazarus (ch. 11). A dialogical structure of the chapter concludes with Jesus' command: "Lazarus, come out" (v. 43). In this seventh sign, Lazarus' illness is inextricably connected with a manifestation of God's glory: God's power working through Jesus' sign (v. 4). According to the narrator, Jesus' hour of glorification begins proleptically since the raising of Lazarus is the catalyst for plotting Jesus' death (11:45-53).

The *dramatis personae* symbolically constitute a full range of responses to Jesus although they can be designated as disciples and others. The unnamed disciples who accompany Jesus play a minor role by misunderstanding his work (vv. 7-10). Martha's belief in Jesus, however, is based on his word (vv. 25-26). Unlike the other disciples, her belief preceded Jesus' sign and enabled her to witness his glory (11:40) as the other disciples had experienced it at Cana (2:11). Martha's comprehensive confession parallels Nathanael's (1:49): "I believe you are the Christ, the Son of God, he who is coming into the world" (v. 27). Her statement is a variation of the Petrine confession at Caesarea Philippi (Matt 16:16 par.). Her confession at Bethany (near Jerusalem) is an additional response which supersedes that of the Galilean official. His belief in Jesus' word was followed by the confirming sign which restored life to his son (4:46-53).

In contrast to her sister Martha, Mary is a secondary, two-dimensional character. She does not advance the drama either by her actions or her speech which are stylized to repeat Martha's character, thereby drawing attention to her significance in the narrative (cf. vv. 20 and 29, 31; 21 and 32). Lazarus, their brother, is the only voiceless character in the narrative. His restoration to life essentially links him with Jesus to the extent that the chief priests also plot his death (12:10-11).

The Jews are "the others" in the narrative. They are generally described in a positive light: consoling Martha and Mary (v. 19); staying with Mary in the house and accompanying her to the grave (v. 31); showing Jesus Lazarus' tomb (v. 34); and acknowledging Jesus' love for Lazarus (v. 36). As the narrative ends with its climax extending into chapter twelve, the description of "the others" changes. Some blame Jesus for not preventing Lazarus' death (v. 37).

The disagreement over Jesus (vv. 36-37) develops. The raising of Lazarus elicited faith from one group who had been present at the tomb (11:34; 12:11). They *witnessed* to Jesus because of his sign (12:17). The tense of the verb *(emarturei)* suggests that their faith in Jesus prompted a continuous witness. Some of those present at the tomb, however, reported Jesus' action to the authorities (11:46). His sign did not lead to belief for them. A third group, "a great crowd," appears in chapter twelve. In Jerusalem for the Passover, they are drawn to Jesus because they have heard about Lazarus (12:12, 18). Although they greet him enthusiastically with palm branches and acclamation (12:13), there is no indication from the narrator of their subsequent belief. The final group described in the narrative, the officials (11:46; 12:10, 19), realize that Jesus' signs are dangerously persuasive: "Everyone will believe in him" (11:47-48; cf. 12:11, 19). This is the group that plots Jesus' death (11:45-57).

Lazarus and Martha are the only individuals in the narrative whom Jesus addresses directly. While Lazarus' response to Jesus' command is not recorded, Martha's response is a confession, a genre appropriate for revelation. How does Jesus identify himself? "I am *(egō eimi)* the resurrection and the life" (v. 25a). His statement which discloses *how* he is the life (vv. 25b-26) is the culmination of the "I am" sayings in the Book of Signs (1:19–12:50).

First, to satisfy the basic needs of hunger and thirst, Jesus himself supplies the nourishment: "I am *(egō eimi)* the bread of life; whoever comes to me shall not hunger, and whoever believes in me will never thirst" (6:35 NAB). The parallelism of "whoever comes to me" and "whoever believes in me" suggests that the believer is sustained and satisfied by Jesus' teaching. This sapiential interpretation for the bread of life is complemented by the Eucharistic interpretation of 6:51-58. In both interpretations, hunger and thirst are negated and life is given in abundance.

Second, to free individuals from final condemnation, Jesus cancels the judgment (3:18). Judgment occurs during an individual's life. Believing in Jesus means participating now in eternal life; conversely, those who do not believe condemn themselves as long as their failure to believe persists.

Third, to dispel the darkness experienced in life, Jesus offers himself as the source of light: "Whoever believes in me may not remain in darkness" (8:12; 9:5, 39). The *present* experience of the believer can also be described by considering 12:46 *in tandem* with 6:37b: "The one who comes to me I will not cast out." The verses contain an element of final judgment imagery—being cast out into the darkness. From the Johannine perspective, the judgment is realized now. No one who believes will be subject to darkness now or eternally.

Fourth, to deal with death itself, Jesus promises that death is not the ultimate condition: "Whoever believes in him should not perish but have eternal life" (3:16b). The death implied in "perish" is clarified in 11:25-26 where physical death is not denied; rather, the assurance of everlasting life beyond the grave is emphasized.

The believer, then, possesses the resources needed to face the experiences which threaten life (hunger and thirst, moral judgment, darkness, and spiritual death). In addition, the believer receives eternal life (3:16, 36). According to 6:40, belief in Jesus is the basis of eternal life while 11:25-26 emphasizes the definitive absence of death for the one who believes. Correspondingly, a refusal to believe means a rejection of life (5:40). Whether or not the noun "life" *(zōē)* is continuously qualified by the adjective "eternal" *(aiōnios)* is not significant since whenever "life" appears in any verse it signifies the life common to the Father and Son which is shared by the believer. Finally, participation in divine life is a present reality for the believer. The Prologue describes this reality: "To those who believed in his name, he gave power to become children of God" (1:12).

The juxtaposition of "I am" *(ego eimi)* sayings with "Son of man" *(ho huios tou anthropou)* sayings in Jesus' revelations about himself as *the* life results in the mutual transformation of the traditions proper to each saying. The result is a startling theological insight for the reader which clarifies and subtly confirms the claim of Jesus about his relationship to the Father: "I and the Father are one" (10:30). Identifications given to Jesus (e.g., Messiah, prophet) by various characters support the insight as a trajectory of names which are also given new possibilities.

i. Episodes before Passover

In light of the extraordinarily developed structure and function of chapter eleven, it is understandable that exegetes consider chapter twelve less remarkable. The chapter is like an open bamboo shade that lets in light not only to refresh the reader's memory about what has already happened but also to offer clues about future developments. The first scene (vv. 1-11) reintroduces individuals from the preceding narrative: Lazarus, Martha, and Mary. In contrast to her previous position, Mary is now the actor who anoints Jesus' feet with her hair (vv. 3-4). While Judas protests the extravagance of the act, Jesus disagrees (vv. 4-8). Having found out that Jesus is in Bethany, a great crowd comes to see Lazarus, also (v. 11).

The scene is heavily weighed down with anticipation of Jesus' hour: "six days before the Passover" (v. 1); "Judas . . . (he who was to betray him)" (v. 4); "Let her keep it for the day of my burial. . . . you do not always have me" (vv. 7-8); "the chief priests planned to put Lazarus also to death" (v. 10). Three actions indicate another level of anticipation: Lazarus being raised from the dead (v. 1); Jesus' feet being anointed (v. 3); the supper at Martha and Mary's where Judas pretends a concern for the poor (v. 5). In the next supper of Jesus and the disciples, when Judas leaves to betray him, some disciples thought he was instructed to give to the poor (13:29b).

Jews who had heard about Jesus' raising of Lazarus are introduced at the end of the scene. Their presence extends the tension underlined by the narrator who remarks: "many of the Jews were turning away and believing in Jesus because of [Lazarus]" (v. 11). Both a Passover crowd having heard about Jesus' activity

(vv. 12, 18) and officials plotting his death (vv. 10, 19) join the crowd for the next scene which occurs on the following day.

Jesus' entry into Jerusalem is acclaimed by a great crowd (vv. 12-15), but it is recorded that many of the disciples did not comprehend the event until after Jesus' glorification (v. 16) while some who had been at Lazarus' tomb with him continued to bear him witness (v. 17). The Pharisees' ironic comment completes the scene: "You see that you can do nothing; look, the world has gone after him" (v. 19).

The first two scenes of chapter twelve with their mixture of past and future references are a prelude to the appearance of new characters who encounter Jesus in the third scene (vv. 20-36). Two spiral techniques laden with irony introduce "some Greeks" *(Hellēnes tines)* who had come to worship at Passover (v. 20). First, during Tabernacles, they had been identified as a group in the Diaspora *(eis tēn diasporan),* probably Gentiles whom Jesus might teach (7:35). Connecting Jesus with the Gentiles was one response of the Jews to Jesus' mysterious language about going where they could not find him (v. 33). While it may signal some derision, the reader knows how ironic the remark is. Jesus' departure is his hour which when accomplished will provide more than teaching for the Greeks. The entrance of some Greeks in chapter twelve collapses the time barrier separating the scenes and signals a new time. Second, the Greeks approached Philip. Here, they are Jewish proselytes among the worshipers at Passover who ask Philip to see Jesus. He, in turn, tells Andrew. Both communicate the message to Jesus. The chain of communication is the reverse of the one which described how the first disciples invited others to come and see Jesus (1:37-45).

Jesus' response to Philip and Andrew is the inauguration of his hour: "The hour has come for the Son of man to be glorified" (12:24). Three short parabolic sayings introduced by "truly, truly, I say" *(amēn, amēn legō)* strengthen the announcement: a) a grain of wheat must fall into the ground and die to bring forth fruit (v. 24); b) one must die to live eternally (v. 25); and c) serving *(diakonē)* Jesus must include following *(akoloutheitō)* him to be where Jesus is (v. 26).

Did the Greeks respond to Jesus' teaching? Did they spend time with him? They may remain as silent witnesses while Jesus continues to teach. His next declaration offers a rare glimpse into his emotions: "Now my soul is troubled. And what shall I say? 'Father, save me from this hour'? No, for this purpose I have come to this hour. Father, glorify thy name" (vv. 27-28a).[43] The statement is a synopsis of the garden narrative of the Synoptic Gospels (Mark 14:32-42, esp. vv. 34-36, par.).

Next, a heavenly voice confirms Jesus' struggle and request: "I have glorified it, and I will glorify it again" (12:28b). A crowd is suddenly introduced in the midst of Jesus' prayer. Could the voice be an angel's or is it thunder? Jesus does not identify the source but assures the crowd that it happened for their sake (vv. 29-30). The confirmation of Jesus' identity by the heavenly voice is similar to what occurred at Jesus' baptism in the Synoptic Gospels: "You are my beloved Son; with you I am well pleased" (Mark 1:11 NAB, par.). The declaration of sonship, however, does not occur in John 12:28b. It is an intentional omission since sonship identifies *the* relationship of Jesus and the Father. In 12:28b, the verbs of glorification to specify past and future activity refer to Jesus as the Logos and Jesus as the Son (cf. 17:1, 4-5, 22, 24). Only the Father's Son can accomplish the hour. Only Jesus as the incarnate Logos would struggle with its demands.

Future glorification will be accomplished through judgment now (v. 31). What Jesus spoke to Nicodemus privately, he now repeats publicly: " And when I am lifted up from the earth, I will draw everyone to myself" (v. 32 NAB; cf. 3:14-15). That "Son of man" and "I" are self-revelatory, equivalent terms is clear from the substitution of "I" for "Son of man" in 12:32. The narrator adds an explanatory note to identify "lifting up" as "the kind of death he was to die" (v. 33 NAB). He also skillfully introduces a question which repeats Jesus' teaching. They know from the law that the Messiah remains always. "How can you

[43]There are only three events which precipitate an emotional response from Jesus in the Fourth Gospel. The events are centered about Jesus' approaching death. In the Lazarus narrative when Jesus saw Mary and the Jews weeping, "He was deeply moved in spirit and troubled" (11:33). After inquiring about where Lazarus is laid, "Jesus wept" (v. 35). The verb *(edakrusen)* occurs only once *(hapax legomenon)* in the New Testament. In approaching the tomb, Jesus is "deeply moved again" (v. 38). The verb for Jesus' perturbation *(tarassō)* in the Lazarus narrative (v. 33) describes his agitation about his hour (12:27). The same verb is used when Jesus foretells his betrayal (13:21) and speaks with his disciples at Supper (14:1, 27).

say that the Son of man must be lifted up? Who is this Son of man?'' (vv. 34-35).

Jesus responds to their questions by commanding them to ''walk while you have the light . . . with you a little longer . . . lest the darkness overtake you. . . . believe in the light'' (vv. 35-36). What is the intent of Jesus' immediate departure, his hiding from them (v. 37)? They may be ironic responses to the narrator's evaluation of Jesus' ministry. Even though Jesus had worked many signs, they did not believe. Isaiah had foretold their response when he proclaimed God as the one who blinded their eyes and hardened their hearts. The judgment, however, does not cast everyone into the darkness. The narrator indicates that even many of the Pharisees believed in Jesus but were afraid to offer public witness. Why? ''they preferred human praise to the glory of God'' (vv. 37-43).

Suddenly, Jesus reappears to summarize his teaching. He identifies himself as the light who speaks what his Father has commanded him to say. Anyone who believes in him believes in the one who sent him. Conversely, anyone who does not believe is condemned by that disbelief (vv. 44-50). The reader remembers Jesus' identification of himself: ''I am *(egō eimi)* the light of the world'' (8:12). The juxtaposition of ''I'' and ''Son of man'' and ''light'' provides a synthesis of the tension building up about Jesus' identity (chs. 8-12). Those who do not believe in Jesus will be cast out and remain in darkness.

j. Summary

The Book of Signs concludes with an invitation to believe in Jesus—to accept him as *the* light and *the* life who provides everything necessary for the one who believes in him. By being lifted up, Jesus as ''I am'' *(egō eimi),* ''Son,'' and ''Son of man'' now gives eternal life to the believer.

3. The Book of Glory (13:1–20:31)

Unlike the Book of Signs (1:19–12:50), the *setting* here is more circumscribed. Jerusalem, indoors and outdoors, is the space within which Jesus moves freely to the fulfillment of his hour.

Jesus had declared the beginning of his hour (12:23) and had begun to teach about its implications (12:24-46). The narrator's statement in 13:1 enables the reader to participate in the plot: "Now before the feast of the Passover, when Jesus knew that his hour had come to depart out of this world to the Father, having loved *(agapēsas)* his own *(tous idious)* who were in the world, he loved them *(ēgapēsen)* to the end *(eis telos)*." The climax of the Passion Narrative is achieved in Jesus' last statement: "it is finished" *(tetelestai,* 19:30a). An overarching unity is achieved by an inclusion technique. "To the end" *(eis telos,* 13:1) and "it is finished" *(tetelestai,* 19:30a) frame the Last Supper and Passion Narrative.

By what means and for whom Jesus is motivated to accomplish his hour are expressed in the first member of the inclusion (13:1). The tense of the verb "love" *(agapēsas/ēgapēsen)* in 13:1 emphasizes the intensity and depth of Jesus' loving. For whom? The identity of "his own" *(tous idious)* is perplexing for the reader who recalls the Prologue. The light had come to "his own" but "his own" did not accept him (1:11). The evaluation of both belief and unbelief among the Jews may mitigate the statement (12:37-43). Are "his own" to be identified with those outside "his own home" (RSV)? Does the phrase identify the disciples gathered at the meal with Jesus, the ones whom he will address as "mine" *(ta ema,* 17:10) and "children" *(ta teknia,* 13:33)?

Whatever may be the intentional ambiguity of "his own," used perhaps to underscore the poignant irony of the situation, another question immediately arises. How does one measure the intense, deep loving articulated by the verbs? The reader may recall an earlier teaching where Jesus declared: "I lay down my life for my sheep" (10:15b). The motivation for Jesus' self-giving is his willingness to obey his Father's command to lay down his life and take it up again (10:17b). "No one takes it from me but I lay it down on my own. I have power to lay it down, and power to take it again" (10:18ab NAB). "My sheep" *(ta probata)* are the ones for whom Jesus lays down his life. Who are they? A polemical dialogue follows the teaching. Jesus accuses the Jews: "You do not believe, because you are not among my sheep" (10:26). Remember that the climax of chapter ten is the Jews' triple attempt to punish Jesus. Is an ironical identification of the "sheep" provided in a later statement of Jesus when he says, "Greater love has no one than this, that one lays down one's life for one's friends" (15:13)?

a. The Last Supper

(1) Betrayal and Fidelity

Numerous references to betrayal are juxtaposed with summons to fidelity in chapter thirteen. The note of Judas' betrayal during the Supper (v. 2) is linked with Jesus' knowledge of his own origin and return to the Father (v. 3). A second note of betrayal frames Jesus' primary action at the Supper (v. 11). This inclusion (vv. 2, 11) adds foreboding which Jesus' simple action of washing the disciples' feet appears to deflect. Nonetheless, the unusual exchange between Jesus and Simon Peter during the washing (vv. 6-10) alerts the reader to other interpretations of the simple ritual traditionally performed for guests by a household servant. What about it is so difficult to understand that Peter doesn't comprehend *now* but will understand *later?* (v. 7) How can this simple act be so essential that Jesus tells Peter that unless he participates in it, "you will have no part in me" (v. 8b)? The footwashing is a symbolic action which prefigures Jesus' suffering and death.

Jesus follows his act of washing their feet with an explanation for the disciples. As teacher, Jesus has given them an example which they must follow (vv. 12-15). Prefacing his remarks with "truly, truly, I say *(amēn, amēn legō),"* he compares the lowly status of servant to that of master, of the one sent to the sender (v. 16). The humility which undergirds Jesus' acceptance of his hour must be what motivates the disciples to follow Jesus. "If you know this, blessed are you if you do it" (v. 17 NAB). A third note of betrayal is linked with Jesus' *first* revelation of himself as I AM *(egō eimi)* to the disciples (vv. 18-19). In previous I AM *(egō eimi)* statements, Jesus had invited Nicodemus and the Jews to believe that when the Son of man is lifted up I AM is revealed (3:13-14; 8:24, 28). Here, the symbolism of the foot washing is identified with the hour of glorification.

A fourth note of betrayal is developed in the Supper dialogue and action. Deeply troubled (see 11:33 above), Jesus announces: "Truly, truly, I say *(amēn, amēn legō)* to you, one of you will betray me" (v. 21). Simon Peter quickly signals to the disciple reclining at Jesus' side to find out from Jesus whom he means: "It is the one to whom I hand the morsel after I have dipped it." After Judas received the morsel, "Satan entered into him. So Jesus said to him, 'What you are going to do, do quickly' . . . and it was night" (vv. 22-28 NAB).

The departure of Judas formally begins Jesus' hour which had already been declared (12:23, 27; 13:1). The description of Judas going out into the "night" enables the reader to remember Jesus as *the* light. Anyone who follows him will not be in darkness (cf. 8:12; 9:41; 11:9-10). Judas' departure is acknowledged with the *final* Son of man saying in the Gospel. "Now is the Son of Man glorified, and in him is God glorified" (13:31). The saying connects the Lazarus narrative with Jesus' impending death (11:4). God's glory, revealed in Jesus' raising of Lazarus, was the catalyst for plotting Jesus' death.

Aware of the "little while" which remains for them, Jesus announces to the disciples that where he is going they cannot come (v. 33). He leaves them one command which will identify them as his disciples: "Love one another. As *(kathōs)* I have loved *(ēgapēsa)* you, so *(kai)* you also should love *(agapate)* one another *(allēlous)*" (v. 34 NAB). The verb in the first part of the verse ("I have loved") describes proleptically the *final* expression of Jesus' love for the disciples while the verb in the second part of the verse ("you should love") identifies the *continuous* loving activity of the disciples toward one another.

"As I have loved you" suggests that Jesus is the source and the model for the disciples' loving. Where did Jesus learn to love? He learned from the Father. "As *(kathōs)* the Father has loved *(ēgapēsen)* me, so *(kagō)* have I loved *(ēgapēsa)* you" (15:9). It is the mutual love of Jesus and the Father which is the paradigm for the mutual love of the disciples and Jesus. Notice that the "as . . . so" *(kathōs/kai)* pattern of 13:34 is repeated in the "as . . . so" *(kathōs/kagō)* of 15:9. The pattern suggests more than just a simple member of a comparison. "As" *(kathōs)* indicates the source and the intensity of the relationship between Jesus and the disciples: "so (inasmuch as, because) have I loved you" (15:9).

"So you should love one another" adds a second relationship for the disciples who are already intimately united to Jesus. To whom are the disciples to direct this love? The Gospel indicates "one another" *(allēlous,* 13:34 [2 times] 15:12, 17). The term explicitly limits the giving and receiving of love to the disciples. Their belief in Jesus separates them from the world, makes them sisters and brothers of Jesus, and allows them to acknowledge God as their Father (20:17). The mutual love of the disciples is not only a participation in the love between the Father and Son; it is also a participation in the love of the Father and Son for the disciples. These unions exist only among believers.

If the primary designation of "one another" is "disciples," is the "outsider" excluded? There is no explicit response in the Gospel. The love of the disciples for one another is emphasized in the Farewell Discourses (chs. 13–17) where there is a particular focus and urgency to express the command of mutual love as *the* quality which defines the disciples. One cannot conclude, however, that the explicit limit of love is also an exclusive one; this would suggest that the love of the Father and Son is limited to believers.

The final note of betrayal concludes chapter thirteen. Simon Peter asks Jesus about his departure, but he does not comment on the command for mutual love (v. 36a). Jesus replies: "Where I am going you cannot follow *(akolouthēsai)* me now; but you shall follow *(akolouthēseis)* afterward" (v. 36b). Compared to the statement in verse 33b, there are two variations. "Come" is replaced by "follow" and "you shall follow afterward" is added. The substitution of "follow" links the statement to Simon Peter's status as a disciple. In particular, the future following may indicate how he will enter into the suffering of Jesus' hour as well as its glorification (cf. 21:19-23). In contrast, for the Jews who do not believe in him, there is no present or future following of Jesus (7:34b; 8:21b).

With bravado, Simon Peter declares his willingness to immediately follow Jesus: "Lord, why cannot I follow you now? I will lay down my life for you" (v. 37). Laying down his life for his friend is not an option for Peter now. Jesus questions his intention with a proleptic statement: "Will you lay down your life for me? Truly, truly I say *(amēn, amēn legō)* to you, the cock will not crow, till you have denied me three times" (v. 38). Simon Peter does not respond.

(2) Farewell Discourses

In contrast to the dialogical structure of chapter thirteen, the next three chapters are monologues where six exchanges with the disciples have been inserted. Categorized as the Farewell Discourses, there is no consensus about specific sources or substructures for the material. One moves *outside* of time and *inside* the hearts of Jesus and the disciples gathered at table. The serenity of the setting is not jarred either by the consistent references to chronological and spatial time or by the declarations of suffering. Themes introduced in the Book of Signs now appear as instructions for the disciples.

Where Jesus is going is a consistent question for the crowds, whether or not it is voiced. Indeed, some of them thought that he intended to commit suicide or go on a mission to the Greeks. His reply, warning the Jews of his departure and the impossibility for them to go with him, terminated the dialogue (see 7:33-36; 8:21-24 above). Whenever the disciples—as for example, Simon Peter—ask Jesus the *same* question during the Supper, however, the dialogue continues. The Gospel writer uses a three-step sequence: revelation (13:33), question (36a, 37), and clarification (13:36b, 38).

In chapter fourteen, the narrator records Jesus' new revelation about his departure. Jesus will return to the Father in order to prepare many dwellings *(monai pollai)* for the disciples (v. 2). The "dwellings" are neither temporary resting places along a journey nor compartments in heaven; rather, they represent a permanent mode of abiding—to be where Jesus and the Father are (v. 3).

How Jesus will attain his goal is introduced in verse 4 where he challenges his disciples to acknowledge that his way will be through suffering and death. Thomas replies with two questions about destination and route which reveal his misunderstanding of the revelation. The situation is parallel to Jesus' assessment of the Jews who misunderstand his origin and destination (8:14b). Here, however, Jesus clarifies his revelation (cf. 8:15-18) by focusing attention on the disciples' destination and route. He answers Thomas' second question first. He is the way (v. 6a) and the exclusive access to the Father (v. 6b). The two nouns which explain "way," i.e., "truth" and "life," indicate how Jesus is the sole means to the Father. Jesus is the "truth" because he is the revelation of the Father. His direct experience of the Father, all that Jesus has seen and heard, is its basis. Jesus is also the "life" because he offers to believers a participation in the life that he shares with the Father (10:10; 14:20).

Then, Jesus responds to Thomas' other question about his destination which is the Father. His revelation contains a promise: "If you had known me (as in fact they do), you would have known my Father also" (14:7a). The revelation also indicates a possibility already within the disciples' grasp: "Henceforth, you know him and have seen him" (14:7b). This statement of possibility and partially realized fact is in striking contrast to the failure of the Jews to know Jesus (8:19). Verse 7 emphasizes that Jesus is the exclusive means of access to the Father for the disciples because knowing and seeing *him* is knowing and seeing the *Father*. Philip, however, who is the next questioner, misunderstands and asks for a direct vision of the Father (v. 8). Once again, Jesus clarifies his message by repeating the significance of their experience: seeing him *is* seeing the Father (v. 9).

Verses 10 and 11 substantiate the unique relationship of Jesus and the Father by identifying the mutual indwelling of Jesus and the Father as *the* relationship which is the basis for Jesus' claims. Mutual indwelling affects everything which Jesus says and does as belonging to the Father. The verses indicate another parallel in the Book of Signs about Jesus' relationship to the Father. In 10:31-38, the Jews' hostile dialogue and intended action focus on Jesus' claim of doing his Father's works (v. 37). He invites the Jews to at least believe in his works if they cannot believe in his person in order that they might acknowledge the mutual indwelling which he shares with the Father. Their response is attempted stoning (v. 31). In 14:10-11, although the reasoning and message are the same, there is no hostility. Verse 11 repeats Jesus' appeal to the disciples to believe in his mutual indwelling with the Father by believing in either Jesus or his works (v. 10).

The fourth exchange between Jesus and the disciples is the longest (14:12-31). It is interrupted by a saying on prayer (v. 13) and two Paraclete sayings (vv. 15b-17, 25-26). The indwelling theme of verses 10-11 is continued in verses 18-21. Jesus promises that although he will leave his disciples, he will not abandon them (v.

18); rather, he will "return." How? Although the world will not see Jesus again after his death, the disciples *will* see him after the resurrection and also share in that event which communicates the life shared by the Father and Jesus (v. 20). Jesus' manifestation of himself to the disciples after the resurrection will be their experience of the mutual indwelling between him and the Father. It results from the loving relationship initiated by the Father and Jesus which is developed by the disciples' fidelity to his word (vv. 20-21).

Judas (not the Iscariot) raises a question based on popular belief about future eschatology: "Lord, how is it that you will manifest yourself to us, and not to the world?" (v. 22). Jesus confirms that after his hour (and because of it) the disciples will enter into a mutual indwelling with him and the Father, an experience of eternal life now (v. 23). The Father and Jesus make their "dwelling" *(monē)* with the disciples, overcoming their fear of Jesus' departure. Peace is an effect of this mutual indwelling (v. 27). The theme of departing and returning is reintroduced as an occasion for the disciples' rejoicing because it is the completion of Jesus' work which is to do what the Father has commanded him to do (vv. 28, 31).

After the parable of the vine and branches and the declaration of the world's hatred for Jesus and the disciples (15:1–16:4a), the theme of Jesus' departure and return reappears (16:5-23a). This exchange, like the previous one, is marked by two Paraclete sayings (vv. 7-11, 12-15). The disciples' anxiety about his departure, to which Jesus had alluded before (14:1), deepens now (16:6, 20-22). Jesus' promise that they will see him again is repeated to transform their sorrow into joy. Jesus begins this revelation with an announcement of his return to the Father and his observation that none of the disciples has asked him where he is going (16:5). In his statement about "going," the verb *(hupagō)* used in 7:33 is repeated frequently in the Farewell Discourses (13:33, 36; 14:4, 5, 28; *16:5)*.

Jesus reiterates his announcement about departure and return in "a little while" (16:16). The time phrase *(mikron)* which heightens the imminent departure of Jesus (13:33; 14:19) also reassures the disciples of Jesus' return. While they will no longer see Jesus' physical presence (cf. v. 10a), the disciples will experience a new type of presence when Jesus returns to them. Although they do not question Jesus, the disciples ask one another what he means by "a little while" and "return to the Father" (vv. 17-18). An inclusion (vv. 16-19) frames Jesus' clarification of the questions he knows they want to ask. He contrasts the non-believers' rejoicing with the disciples' grieving (v. 20). Drawing on the imagery of childbirth, Jesus promises the disciples that he will return, transforming their grief into joy, a joy which no one will snatch away (vv. 21-22). "On that day" there will be no need for further questions (v. 23a).

Characteristically, Jesus' clarification raises more questions. When will Jesus come again? How will he return? Similar to the previous exchange (14:12-31), there are two foci. First, the resurrection will bring them joy and revelation. In addition, a more permanent presence than post-resurrection appearances is indicated by the descriptions of lasting joy, knowledge, and fulfilled petitions (vv. 22b-24). Second, the indwelling presence of Jesus and the Father announced earlier (14:19-23) is appropriate here. The repetition of the phrase "on that day" (14:20; *16:23)* identifies the beginning of a new, lasting relationship of Jesus and the Father with the disciples. The theme of realized eschatology also functions in the childbirth imagery which is a prophetic analogy for the ushering in of the final age. In particular, the suffering imagery describes the tribulation which precedes God's eschatological action for the people (see Dan 12:1 [LXX]; Hab 3:16; Zeph 1:14-15). As developed here, the disciples' tribulation at Jesus' departure precedes their vindication and joy—their experience of his permanent presence after the resurrection. Their intimacy with Jesus and the Father is the reason why their requests are answered (vv. 23-24).

In 16:25-33, the final exchange develops. Jesus promises the disciples that the hour is coming when he will speak to them plainly *(parrēsia),* not in parables *(paroimiai),* about the Father. The clause "the hour is coming" refers to a post-resurrection time when they will grasp Jesus' revelation (v. 25). There is a parallel between this clear revelation about the Father and Jesus' promise of "heavenly things" *(epourania)* to Nicodemus (3:12). Understanding "heavenly things" is precarious in the disciples' *present* circumstances. The reader, however, understands it as a comprehensive experience of the Father in Jesus.[44] In contrast, understanding "heavenly things" is denied to Nicodemus who neither grasps Jesus' teaching nor attains the same depth of believing as the disciples. The parallel is another example of the repetition of themes introduced in the Book of Signs and clarified through instruction in the Book of Glory.

Revelation about the Father continues (16:26-28). Praying in Jesus' name gives the disciples confidence that the Father will hear them because of the mutual love between them, Jesus, and the Father. The phrase "on that day" indicates the relationship initiated after the resurrection (v. 26). Jesus' ministry affects the relationship: "I came from the Father and have come into the world; again, I am leaving the world and going to the Father" (v. 28). This time the disciples do not intervene with a question. Instead, their remarks have a subtle irony because of their facile assumption that they understand Jesus' speaking plainly *(parrēsia)*. There is no need for a parable *(paroimia)*. It is not necessary to ask Jesus any questions because they know he has come from God. Nevertheless, they fail to understand his revelation about the necessity for his departure.

Jesus' clarification begins with a direct question about the disciples' believing, repeating the irony of their intervention (v. 31). The clause "the hour is coming" is repeated (v. 32) to stress the imminence of Jesus' approaching hour when the disciples will desert him. The Farewell Discourses, however, conclude on a positive note with Jesus' assurance that the Father is always with him (v. 32; cf. 8:29). Jesus again offers the disciples his peace which arises from the anticipation of his completed hour (v. 33).

(3) Jesus' Prayer

Chapter seventeen describes Jesus' prayer to the Father. It is his concluding words—perhaps his ultimate disclosure—to the disciples at the supper table. While Jesus had prayed for himself (see 12:27, 28a) and taught the disciples about prayer (14:13-14; 15:7a; 16:23-24, 26), here the structure of the prayer provides a synthesis of thought unparalleled in the Gospel. The prayer con-

---

[44]J. Terence Forestell, *The Word of the Cross: Salvation as Revelation (AnBib* 57; Rome: Pontifical Biblical Institute, 1974) 41.

sists of six petition and six review units which follow one another in a consistent pattern.[45] In the petition units, Jesus asks his Father for his own glorification (vv. 1-3, 5) and for the needs of his disciples (vv. 9-11, 15-17, 20-21, 24) whereas in the review units he enumerates his past accomplishments and circumstances (vv. 4, 6-8, 12-14, 18-19, 22-23, 25-26).

Although Jesus' petitions for himself are a repetition of previous prayer, his requests for the disciples are new and numerous. They include a continual relationship with the Father (v. 11); protection from evil (v. 15); and sanctification in the truth (v. 17). The most frequent petition, however, is for unity not only among the disciples themselves (vv. 11, 21) but also with Jesus and the Father (vv. 21, 24). The mutual abiding of Jesus and the Father is the model for Jesus and the disciples: "so that they may all be one as *(kathōs)* you, Father, are in me and *(kagō)* I in you, that they also may be in us" (v. 21ab NAB). Note that the "as . . . and (so)" *(kathōs/kai)* pattern which identified the mutual loving of Jesus and the Father (15:9) also indicates their mutual abiding.

The relationship of Jesus and the Father, however, is not limited to being a paradigm for the disciples' consideration. Their relationship is essentially significant because it is the source and cause of the unity between the disciples and Jesus, between the disciples with one another. The prayer of Jesus is not primarily concerned with the unity among the disciples. Its first focus is the unity of believers with Jesus and the Father (vv. 21, 23a). How is that unity described? "I wish that where I am they also may be with me, that they may see my glory that you gave me" (v. 24ab NAB; cf. 14:3). Jesus' petition sums up the departure-and-return theme developed in the Last Discourses (chs. 14–16) and adds a new dimension. To be with Jesus and experience his glory (accessible through the completion of his hour) is to breathe the very life breath of Jesus and the Father.

Nonetheless, the experience does not exist for itself as a mystical union. The disciples are enjoined to "bear fruit" (15:2 [two times], 4, 5, 8, 16). This enigmatic command is lived out in a com-

---

[45]M. L. Appold, *The Oneness Motif in the Fourth Gospel: Motif Analysis and Exegetical Probe into the Theology of John (WUNT* 2/1; Tübingen: Mohr-Siebeck, 1976) 227.

munity where the disciples' experience of eternal life is a basis for apostolic activity: witnessing and sharing with others *in* and *outside* the community. To love others according to Jesus' example transforms the individual and the community. It is concurrent with apostolic mission. The second focus of Jesus' prayer for unity, then, is how it becomes present in the community. It is a spiritual gift to be confined within the limits of the believing community as well as a concrete expression of the union of the Father and Son present in the community because of its shared faith and love. This unity is the catalyst for the world's possible conversion, for its belief in and knowledge of Jesus as the one sent by God (vv. 21b, 23b).

(4) Drama of the Son of man

What happened at the Supper where Jesus and the disciples gathered? The narrator constructed the event to offer different levels of meaning. The reader is free to appropriate them according to personal experience and intuition. Is anything new revealed about the Son of man? Textual evidence would appear to rule out that possibility since only one saying about the Son of man appears (13:31) in the first five chapters of the Book of Glory.[46] Nonetheless, the drama of the Son of man unfolds throughout the chapters.

First, there is extraordinary irony in the portrayal of Jesus' departure which is, in fact, his double return, both to the Father and to the disciples. While chronological and spatial indicators are used to describe the process, they point to a new reality. Jesus' departure and return through the passage of his hour forge new relationships which connect Jesus, the Father, and the disciples in mutualities beyond imagining. The Son of man in being "lifted up" draws believers to himself, the Father, and each other to share one life which begins now and lasts forever.

Second, Jesus as the revelation of the Father loves his own to the end (13:1). As a vision of the Father, he expresses in what he says and does the relationship from which he draws his being: mutual knowing, loving, and abiding with the Father (10:15; 15:9; 17:21). He invites the disciples to enter into the same relation-

---

[46]Cf. Maddox, 93, 202–3.

ship which he shares with the Father. That the invitation is a matter of choice is indicated through characters who refuse it. Both
in the betrayal of Jesus by Judas and then by Peter, motivations
are secondary to the denial of the relationship. In contrast, motivations for future choices are described. The world (nonbelievers)
will hate and persecute the disciples because they do not belong
to them (15:18-19). Others will also persecute the disciples whose
motivation is "offering service to God" (16:2). The loving and
abiding that are integral to mutual relationships are the antitheses
of betraying and denying them. Mutual relationships participate
in divine glory while betrayal and denial cast individuals into
darkness.

Third, how Jesus is named in chapters thirteen, fourteen, and
seventeen anticipates the motivations for his opponents' activities in the Passion Narrative. Although he is seldom called "Son"
(14:13; 17:1 [2 times], 12), it is only as Son that Jesus' promises
will be fulfilled. He refers to himself as "I am" *(egō eimi,* 13:19)
and "Son of man" (13:31). He uses both identifications for himself in the context of betrayal. Earlier, these claims of identity
were denied by crowds and only affirmed by a few individuals.
At this juncture in the drama, even the firm conviction of the disciples is shaken when two of their own betray Jesus. It is as
"Son," "Son of man," and "I am" that Jesus' final instructions
and prayer are given authenticity and power.

b. The Passion Narrative

In contrast to the supper setting of the previous chapters, the
settings change often in the Passion Narrative (18:1-19:42). From
the moment that Jesus and the disciples leave *(exēlthen)* the room
and enter *(eisēlthen)* the Kidron valley and garden (18:1), there
will be a constant influx of characters who interact with them in
settings that shift from outdoors to indoors. Characters are also
deeply cast in ironic comments and acts. These intentional literary techniques of the narrator provide a broad basis for provok-
ing interest and suspense in a tightly scripted time sequence about
the final outcome of Jesus.

(1) Jesus' Arrest and Interrogation

Section One of the Passion Narrative presents the arrest and
interrogation of Jesus (18:1-27; cf. Matt 26:47-75 par.). Judas who

had departed *(exēlthen)* after eating the morsel given to him by Jesus during the night (13:30) reenters the drama by arriving in the garden. In contrast to the past serenity of the location where Jesus "often met with his disciples," now Judas approaches with "a band of soldiers, some officers from the chief priests and the Pharisees," as well as "lanterns and torches and weapons" (v. 3). Note the emphasis on implements to provide light. Judas and his accomplices are in more than physical darkness, yet they seek Jesus, the light of the world (8:12).

Jesus takes the initiative in approaching them with the quintessential question: "Whom do you seek?" (v. 4). "Jesus the Nazarene," they reply (v. 5). The reader remembers Jesus' same question to two disciples of the Baptizer. While they had addressed Jesus as "Rabbi," a title similar to his given name in 18:5, they had asked Jesus a question: "Where are you staying?" Jesus replied: "Come and see" (1:38-39). In the garden, Jesus' answer to his questioners is more direct: "I am he *(egō eimi)*" (18:5b). While the first disciples responded to Jesus by following him and staying with him (1:39), this group "drew back and fell to the ground" (18:6). Jesus' self-revelation is ironically his given name. The narrator acknowledges the reply, "I am he *(egō eimi),*" by the group's physical response—a prostration in the presence of a theophany, another ironic touch. The dialogue is repeated again with Jesus' insistence, "If you seek me, let these men go" (vv. 7-8). Peter responds to Jesus' being apprehended by the soldiers by cutting off a servant's ear (v. 10), but Jesus declares: "Shall I not drink the cup which the Father has given me?" (v. 11b). His serenity in knowing what will happen (v. 4) and his statement to Peter (v. 11b) offer the reader a vivid contrast to the characters assembled in the garden.

The depiction of Jesus and Peter in the conclusion of the garden scene is developed in the next two split scenes where both Jesus and Peter are interrogated simultaneously by different persons. A transitional commentary describes Jesus being led *(ēgagon)* to Annas' chambers and comments on Caiaphas' statement about having one man die for the people (vv. 12-14; cf. 11:49-53). In the first split scene, side a, Peter, who was outside *(echō)* the courtyard, was let in *(eisēgagen)* by the gatekeeper who inquired whether he was not one of "this man's *(anthrōpou toutou)* dis-

ciples." Peter answered her: "I am not" (vv. 15-17). Side b
presents Annas' investigation of Jesus' disciples and teaching.
Jesus, however, tells him to question those who heard him preach
since he has taught openly in both temple and synagogue. A sol-
dier responds by striking Jesus (cf. v. 10). After he questioned
the blow, Jesus is sent to Caiaphas (vv. 19-23). The reader perceives the irony of a disciple cowering before a gatekeeper who
is also a woman while Jesus orders Annas to ask his disciples about
him. In the second split scene, side a, Peter again is described first.
Guards standing around a fire (v. 18) question his affiliations.
One of the high priest's servants, a relative of the servant whose
ear Peter had severed, immediately repeats their question. Twice
Peter denies his identity as Jesus' disciple: "I am not" (vv. 25-27).

(2) Jesus' Encounters with Pilate and the Jews

Section Two of the Passion Narrative describes Jesus' encounters with Pilate and the Jews (18:28–19:16a; cf. Matt 27:1-2,
11-31a par.). It begins with the second split scene, side b, com-
posed of several dialogues. Having led *(agousin)* Jesus to the
praetorium (v. 28), the Jews demanded that Pilate judge Jesus'
situation. They refused to enter the praetorium, a Roman judi-
cial seat, "so that they might not be defiled, but might eat the
Passover" (v. 28b). Pilate went out *(exēlthen . . . echō)* to them:
"What accusation do you bring against this man *(anthrōpou toutou)?*" They retort: "If this man were not an evildoer, we would
not have handed him over" (v. 29). Pilate demands that they settle
the issue according to their own law, but Jewish law forbids the
death penalty (vv. 31-32). Note the irony of judgment and Passover which links the Jews with Jesus.

Pilate again enters *(eisēlthen . . . palin)* the praetorium (v. 33)
as an intermediary between Jesus and the Jews. While he had referred to Jesus as "this man" *(anthrōpou toutou)* before the Jews
(v. 29), now he asks Jesus if he is the "king of the Jews" (v. 33).
Initially, Jesus refuses to answer. After a question regarding his
activity, he responds three times that his kingship is not of this
world (vv. 34-36). When Pilate asks if he is a king, Jesus acknowledges the identification but clarifies his role: "I have come into
the world to bear witness to the truth. Everyone who is of the
truth hears my voice" (v. 37).

Pilate goes out of the praetorium again *(palin exēlthen)* and declares to the Jews that he considers Jesus innocent. Reminding them of a Passover custom to release one prisoner, he suggests the release of the "king of the Jews." The Jews prefer Barabbas (vv. 38b-40). Inside again, Pilate orders that Jesus be scourged (19:1). The soldiers, unlike the Jews, ironically acknowledge Jesus' kingship with a crown of thorns, a purple robe, and the acclamation, "Hail, king of the Jews," while continually striking him (vv. 2-3). Going outside again *(exēlthen palin echō)*, Pilate informs the Jews that he is bringing *(agō)* Jesus out to them because he is innocent. In contrast to Pilate's movement back and forth between Jesus and the Jews, Jesus comes out *(exēlthen echō)* for the first time, adorned with crown and robe. "Behold the man *(ho anthrōpos),"* Pilate declares (vv. 4-5). Even this identification of Jesus (cf. 18:39) brings no resolution for the Jews. Ironically, it is the chief priests and officers who cry out for a conclusion: "Crucify him! Crucify him" (v. 6; cf. 11:47-48). Pilate, however, asserts Jesus' innocence for the third time (18:38; 19:4, 6). Informing Pilate again about their law, the Jews claim that Jesus "made himself the Son of God *(huiou theou),"* a crime punishable by death (19:7).

Frightened, Pilate again enters *(eisēlthen . . . palin)* the praetorium to question Jesus: "Where are you from?" (v. 9). Affronted by Jesus' silence, Pilate informs him that as procurator he has power to release as well as to crucify him. Jesus, however, claims that the power has been given him from above *(anōthen)*. Repeatedly, Pilate has sought Jesus' release by speaking to the Jews. Now they accuse him of not being Caesar's friend: "Everyone who makes himself a king sets himself against Caesar" (vv. 10-12). Once more, Pilate brings Jesus outside *(ēgagen echō)*, places him on the "judgment seat" during Preparation Day for Passover, and declares to the Jews for the third time: "Behold your king!" The Jews, in turn, respond for the second time: "Crucify him!" Pilate gives them one more opportunity: "Shall I crucify your King?" This time, the chief priests who have initiated the cry for crucifixion, proclaim their own fate: "We have no king but Caesar." Jesus, too, is condemned by being handed over to be crucified (vv. 13-16a). The irony of judgment and Passover linking the Jews and Jesus reaches its climax.

(3) Jesus' Crucifixion and Burial

Section Three of the Passion Narrative (19:16b-42; Matt 27:31b-61 par.) offers an interpretation of Jesus' crucifixion and burial in a setting outside Jerusalem. The reader might anticipate more physical details of Jesus' crucifixion (v. 18), given the previous references to the soldiers' striking and scourging him (18:22; 19:1, 3), as well as the vigorous cries of the people for his death (19:6, 15). The reader, however, is introduced to other details. Pilate's function as promoter of Jesus' kingship is completed when he orders an inscription for the cross to be written in Hebrew, Latin, and Greek: "Jesus of Nazareth, King of the Jews." While the chief priests try to tell Pilate that it is only Jesus' name for himself, not theirs, Pilate refuses to capitulate (vv. 16b-22). While Jesus' garments and tunic are divided among the soldiers, a few women witness the event: "his mother, and his mother's sister, Mary the wife of Clopas, and Mary Magdalene" (v. 25). He addresses his mother and the Beloved Disciple as "mother" and "son" to signify their new relationships (vv. 23-26). An inclusion technique (vv. 28, 30) highlights Jesus' imminent death: "knowing that all was finished *(tetelestai)*" and "it is finished *(tetelestai)*." Jesus' suffering and death, which constitute part of his hour, are over.

Afterwards, the legs of the two who had been crucified on either side of Jesus were broken to hasten their deaths on the Preparation Day before the Passover. Jesus' body, however, was not disturbed. Instead, it was given to Joseph of Arimathea who had petitioned Pilate for it. Nicodemus accompanied him to prepare Jesus' body for burial. An extraordinary amount of spices ("a mixture of myrrh and aloes about a hundred pounds' weight") and the linen cloths signify an unusual burial for a crucified person (vv. 31-33, 38-42).

(4) Jesus' Identity

In Sections One and Two of the Passion Narrative, acceptance and rejection of identities is the basic framework for plot development. In Section One, there is the juxtaposition of two opposite identities: the "I am" *(ego eimi)* of Jesus and the "I am not" of Peter. That "Jesus the Nazarene" *is* "I am" *(ego eimi)* overwhelmed the crowd in the garden who worshiped at his feet. That being called "this man's *(anthrōpou toutou)* disciple" over-whelmed Peter, too, is evident through his denial and absence from the narrative after the cock crows.

In Section Two, mutually hostile characters—Pilate and the Jews—engage in naming Jesus. Pilate identifies Jesus as "this man," "the man," and preferably, "king of the Jews."[47] The Jews deny that Jesus is "Son of God" and the "king of the Jews." They call him an "evildoer" and prefer Barabbas, the robber. Ironically, the Jews are forced to rely on the Roman presence represented by Pilate to accomplish the punishment decreed by their own law. Inspired by their religious leaders, the Jews compromise their religious tradition of nearly one thousand years which acclaimed God as king by acknowledging no king but Caesar. While the Roman soldiers and Pilate confirm Jesus' kingship, Jesus transforms their notion of king by identifying a king as one who bears witness to the truth.

In Section Three, the consistent question about Jesus' identity as "king of the Jews" is resolved. For the narrator, Jesus' cross is the enthronement of the king where all people (Jews, Romans, and Greeks) see the revelation of God in the Son of man. He had been dressed with crown and robe by soldiers whose actions are ironic comments on his kingship. Nor after his death is Jesus' body dishonored by being broken; rather, given the circumstances of his death, the extraordinary ritual materials used in anointing and wrapping his body bear a final testimony to the "king of the Jews."

c. Post-resurrection Appearances

Jesus completes his hour in the post-resurrection appearances which constitute the final development of the Book of Glory

---

[47]Francis J. Moloney *(Johannine Son of Man,* 204), commenting on the continual use of motion verbs (28:38–19:16a), divides the drama into seven scenes which form a chiasm highlighting the importance of the kingship motif. The design of the chiasm is:

A: Outside (18:28-32) Jews demand Jesus' death.
B: Inside (18:33-38a) Pilate questions Jesus about *kingship.*
C: Outside (18:38b-40) Jesus is not guilty. The Jews ask for Barabbas instead of *King* of Jews.
D: Inside (19:1-3) Jesus is scourged, clothed, and crowned as *king.*
C¹: Outside (19:4-8) Jesus is not guilty. Behold the man . . . crucify him."
B¹: Inside (19:9-11) Pilate questions Jesus about power.
A¹: Outside (19:12-16a) Jews obtain Jesus' death.

(20:1-24; cf. Matt 28:1-20 par.). The setting moves from the garden tombs area where the Passion Narrative concluded to a locked room in Jerusalem. A few named characters who had been involved in the plot reappear. The generic term "disciples" *(mathē-tēs)* is also used to designate the post-resurrection group. While there is a chronological and spatial limitation of eight days, the reader is aware of Jesus and the characters participating in different time frames.

A literary pattern of claim and response introduced in the Book of Signs functions in the post-resurrection appearances. In the parable of the the shepherd and its midrashic expansion (10:1-5, 11b-13, 14-18), Jesus claims his sheep by naming them and leading them forth. The flock responds by recognizing and following him. The possibility of a new relationship for believers is based on the relationship of Jesus and the Father: "I am the good shepherd; I know my own and my own know me, as *(kathōs)* the Father knows me and *(kai)* I know the Father" (10:14b-15a). Remember how incensed the Jews were when Jesus continued his claims about his relationship with the Father. He indicted them: "You do not believe, because you do not belong to my sheep. My sheep hear my voice, and I know them, and they follow me" (10:22-39, esp. vv. 26-27). The reader recalls Jesus' statement to Pilate: "Everyone who is of the truth hears my voice" (18:37c).

(1) In a Garden

Return now to the first post-resurrection scene in the garden where Jesus was buried (20:1-18). It presents two distinctive episodes which are dependent upon each other. In the first episode, Mary Magdalene who had stood at the foot of the cross (19:25) came to the tomb and saw the stone rolled back. Having run to Simon Peter and the Beloved Disciple, she reported the loss: "They have taken away *(ēran)* the Lord out of the tomb and we do not know *(ouk oidamen)* where they have laid him *(pou ethē-kan auton)*" (vv. 1-2). It is not clear if she expects them to assist her in the search to find Jesus' body.

Mary Magdalene disappears abruptly from the scene to allow the reader to focus full attention on Simon Peter and the Beloved Disciple who become the characters in the second episode. Both run toward the tomb, but the Beloved Disciple arrives first. Peering in, he waits to enter until after Simon Peter arrives and enters. There, they find the linen cloths and the head napkin lying in separate places (vv. 3-7). While neither disciple speaks, the Beloved Disciple "saw and believed" (v. 8). The narrator adds: "As yet they did not know the scripture, that he must rise from the dead" (v. 9). When the disciples return home, the tomb area is empty (v. 10).

The second episode confirms Mary Magdalene's earlier discovery. Does the second episode present anything new? Paul Minear, who radically reinterprets verse 8, limits the "seeing and believing" of the Beloved Disciple to the evidence of the empty grave and burial wrappings. He argues that the disciples' ignorance of the Scripture regarding Jesus' resurrection has no meaning if the Beloved Disciple "saw and believed" in the resurrection at that moment (v. 9); the disciples' departure to their homes excludes faith in the resurrection when compared with the Synoptic Gospels which do not suggest indifference; and descriptions of the risen Jesus' first appearances and the disciples' responses appear to preclude another "first" confession of faith.[48] Two features of characterization utilizing the claim and response pattern support his conclusion. Simon Peter had denied Jesus' claim and had not responded to him after having denied him three times in the courtyard. Although the Beloved Disciple had faithfully stood at the cross (19:25-27), he had not heard the voice of the risen Jesus. There can be no response without a prior claim.

Mary Magdalene re-enters to resume the plot. Weeping, she stands outside the tomb and then peers inside (v. 11). Two angels are seated where the body *(sōma)* of Jesus had been. The reader is surprised, too, since the disciples had found only burial wrappings in the same place. In describing the precise position of the angels, the narrator emphasizes why Mary is searching. When the angels ask her why she is weeping, she repeats the same statement which she had delivered to the disciples (vv. 12-13). Turning around, she sees Jesus but does not recognize him. After echoing the angels' query, Jesus adds his own question: "Woman, why are you weeping? Whom do you seek?" Thinking he is the gardener, she speaks about her search again: "Sir, if you have car-

---

[48]Paul Minear, " 'We Don't Know Where. . .' John 20:2" *Int* 30 (1976) 125-39.

ried him away, tell me where you have laid him *(pou ethēkas auton),* and I will take him away *(arō)"* (vv. 14-15).

Mary Magdalene engaged in three conversations while trying to find Jesus' body. Her weeping and the loss of Jesus' body are consistent elements in her announcements to the disciples, angels, and Jesus (13-15). Since she misunderstood his identity, Jesus takes the initiative to end her search. He calls her by name: "Mary," and she recognizes him as her teacher, "Rabboni" (v. 16; cf. 10:4). In knowing both Jesus' absence (vv. 2, 13, 15) and his presence, Mary clings to him. If the episode concluded here, there would be a clear pattern of claim and response. The episode would mirror two other encounters where Jesus addressed the same question, first to two followers of the Baptizer and then to the crowd in the garden: "What [or Whom] do you seek?" (1: 38; 18:4). One group responded by following Jesus while the other group seized him for crucifixion.

Although there is a proleptic climax to the episode in the garden where there is mutual recognition between Jesus and the woman, what follows surpasses any expectations of either Mary Magdalene or the reader. Jesus commands her: "Do not hold me for I have not yet ascended to the Father; but go to my brethren *(adelphous)*[49] and say to them, 'I am ascending to my Father and your Father, to my God and your God.' Mary Magdalene went and said to the disciples, 'I have seen the Lord'; and she told them that he had said these things to her" (vv. 17-18).

In connecting the resurrection to the ascension, Jesus indicates that his relationship to Mary Magdalene will be different. His return to the Father, to be where he dwells, is another moment of the hour in which he is glorified. The theological rather than chronological and spatial intention of verse 17 also indicates the new relationship which the disciples will enjoy with the risen Jesus and the Father. Jesus' hour of glorification enables the disciples to be children of the Father and brothers and sisters of Jesus. As the first witness of the resurrection, Mary Magdalene responds to Jesus' new claim on her. She fulfills her commission by identifying Jesus for the disciples with new understanding.

---

[49]"Brethren" (RSV) and "brothers" (NAB) for *adelphous* are contrary to the egalitarian nature of the Johannine community. Here "my brothers and sisters" is preferable etymologically and theologically.

(2) In a room

The second post-resurrection appearance occurs the same evening (20:19-23). The setting is stark. Anxious disciples cower behind a locked door, bound together by fear of the Jews (v. 19a). Taking the initiative, Jesus appears and offers the disciples his peace and presence (vv. 19b-20a). Fears fade into the shadows of the waning day as they rejoice in his return (v. 20b). He reassures them that they are not orphans (cf. 16:22) and offers them not only an unimaginable gift but also a responsibility. He equates their future with the role his Father entrusted to him: "As *(kathōs)* the Father has sent me, even so *(kagō)* I send you" (v. 21). Jesus' mission of proclaiming God's truth becomes their mission. They are charged to continue Jesus' revelation of the Father. They are challenged to live out their decision to believe in Jesus by loving one another as Jesus and the Father love both one another *and* the disciples (15:9, 12b).

How will they accomplish this witness and this task? Jesus breathes upon them and says: "Receive the Holy Spirit. If you forgive the sins of any, they are forgiven; if you retain the sins of any, they are retained" (vv. 22-23). Jesus' hour has now been definitively completed. He has returned to renew his relationship to the disciples by means of commissioning, the insufflation of his Spirit, and directives to be reconcilers.

There is no indication of the disciples' immediate response to Jesus' appearance (v. 20). Eight days later, however, the third post-resurrection scene describes how the disciples' experience of Easter evening was challenged from within their own community (vv. 24-29). Thomas had not shared their experience. Incredulous, he declared: "Unless I see in his hands the print of the nails, and place my finger in the mark of the nails, and place my hand in his side, I will not believe" (v. 25). When Jesus appears the third time, he invites Thomas to see for himself and to believe. Overcome, Thomas addresses Jesus: "My Lord and my God." Jesus' blessing is not for Thomas; rather, it is for "those who have not seen and yet believe" (vv. 26-29). The scene describes another example of claim and response whose variation is central to the witness of the Gospel.

(3) Additional identity

Compared to the rich diversity of names used to identify Jesus in the Passion Narrative, it may be surprising to note that the post-resurrection appearances use only a few terms: Rabbi, Lord, Messiah, and Son of God. "Rabbi" (v. 16) is a designation familiar to the reader from the Book of Signs. The disciples consistently address Jesus as "Teacher" (1:38, 49; 4:31; 9:2; 11:8; cf. 3:2, 26; 6:25). "Lord" *(kurios)* which occurs on the lips of characters and narrator alike identifies Jesus. It is used either in a respectful form of direct address—"Sir" and "Lord" (RSV) or "Master" (NAB) (4:11, 15, 19, 49; 5:7; 6:34, 68; 9:36; 11:3, 12, 21, 32, 34, 39; 12:21; 13:6, 9, 25, 36, 37; 14:5, 8, 22; 20:15)—or in a report *about* him (6:23; 11:2; 20:2, 13, 20, 25). The narrator also cites Scripture in which "Lord" occurs (1:23; 12:13, 38). Jesus uses "Lord" in affirming the disciples' identification of him (13:13, 14, 16; 15:15, 20).

There are also uses of "Lord" *(kurios)* on the lips of disciples which may identify Jesus in a fuller way. Two narratives in the Book of Signs may indicate a post-resurrection understanding of Jesus as "Lord" from the perspective of the Johannine community. After the man born blind was expelled from the synagogue, Jesus questioned him about whether he believed in the Son of man. After receiving Jesus' clarification, he confesses: " 'Lord, I believe'; and he worshiped him" (9:38). Martha also acknowledges who Jesus is after his teaching on the resurrection: "Yes, Lord; I believe that you are the Christ, the Son of God, he who is coming into the world" (11:27). Similarly, in the Book of Glory there are also two post-resurrection narratives where the meaning of "Lord" is probably more than "Sir." Mary Magdalene as the herald of the resurrection proclaims: "I have seen the Lord" (20:18). Thomas, whose faith is deepened by his experience of the risen Jesus, confesses: "My Lord and my God" (20:28; cf. 21:7, 16, 17).

The final declaration about Jesus occurs in the conclusion to the Book of Glory. The narrator states that the Gospel has been written to invite people to believe or keep on believing that "Jesus is the Christ, the Son of God, and that believing they may have life in his name" (20:30-31). Some of the uses of "Christ/Messiah" in the Gospel are ambiguous and do not function as titles.[50] "Messiah" is not the most important name for Jesus. Another name which appears in confessional contexts is "Son of God" on the lips of the Baptizer (1:34), Nathanael (1:49), Martha (11:27), and the narrator (20:31). Jesus also used the phrase (3:18; 5:25; 11:4). Some of the angry crowd had also pointed Jesus out first to one another (10:36) and then to Pilate (19:7) Jesus' admission that he was the Son of God.

d. Synthesis

The results obtained from analyzing the explicit names given to Jesus in the Book of Glory are neither satisfactory nor conclusive. The narrator's most frequent name for Jesus is "Jesus," and for God it is "Father." In addition, the preference for "Son" is quite clear: "Son" without modifiers; "Son" with the adjective "only (begotten) *(monogenēs)*" (1:14 [implicit], 3:17, 18); 'Son' as the subject of two phrases—"Son of God" and "Son of man." Structurally, too, there are clues about the function of "Son." Since it occurs thirty-three times in the Book of Signs compared to four times in the Book of Glory, its function is clearly in settings involving controversy rather than in instructions to the community.[51]

In the Fourth Gospel, Jesus' relationship to God is most clearly and repeatedly described as that of the only *(monogenēs)* Son of the Father. That Jesus is the perfect revelation of the Father is developed through the unity which characterizes the relationship and which is expressed through mutual relationships of knowing, loving, and abiding wherein Jesus continues his Father's works. The Gospel is a witness to how Jesus as the Father's Son also functions discretely as the Son of man in ways considered revolutionary when compared to Jewish tradition.

---

[50]The only example of a reverse in translation for *Christos,* i.e., "Christ" (RSV) and "Messiah" (NAB) occurs in 20:31 (see above, n. 38). It may signify a difference in meaning, for the translators may be influenced by later Christological titles.

[51]Robin Scroggs, *Christology in Paul and John* (Proclamation Commentaries; Fortress: Philadelphia, 1988), 67–68.

Part Three: The Son of Man and New Testament Christologies

This section examines the relationship of the Fourth Gospel as story (Part Two) to New Testament Christologies. The fundamental question of method for biblical interpretation and Christology is addressed through a survey of contemporary perspectives on methodology. Dissatisfaction with the method employed in titular Christology prompted the development of other methods: the new search for the historical Jesus, social-historical analysis, narrative theory, and literary criticism. Next, there is a review of scholarship about the function and relationship of the Johannine Son of man sayings to the Christology of the Fourth Gospel. My interpretation of the implications of the Fourth Gospel as story for Johannine Christology concludes the section.

Contemporary Perspectives

Scholars today frequently discuss how to construct and use responsible methods for investigating New Testament Christologies. They are also aware that they must not only dismiss the possibility of being objective but must also be very clear about how their individual hermeneutical biases can affect the investigation since there is an integral connection between these two conditions and the images of Jesus which emerge.

The methodological discussions developed, in part, from a dissatisfaction with titular Christology where the names given to Jesus or used by him were assessed for their provenance and chronological development. Two presuppositions concerning this method were its objectivity and its goal—an interpretation of the person and event of Jesus through the titles attributed to him. As Leander E. Keck commented, the method was unsatisfactory since the titles in their pre-Christian tradition (except for "prophet") were not appropriate for the hermeneutical task. Neither have scholars been able to substantiate the fact that Jesus applied the "titles" to himself. Furthermore, the Jesus event ought to be the interpreter of the titles and not vice versa.[52] Another criticism of titular Christology is the presupposition of reconstructing and identifying communities as the locus for particular titles. Both evaluations underscore the tendency to isolate verses as representative of the entire text. Although the popularity of the titular approach is waning, it may have successors who study a Gospel to discover within it conflicting Christological statements which are attributed to particular communities.[53]

The process involved in the new search for the historical Jesus is indicative of one approach to New Testament Christologies. (See above, The Focus of the Synoptic Gospels: Evaluation). There are two other prominent ones which assist an interpreter to expand the horizons of personal hermeneutics for the exegetical task. In social-historical analysis, scholars seek to correlate the Christology of a Gospel with the community involved in its composition by examining the role of the disciples. Wayne Meeks, Gerd Theissen, Howard Clark Kee, and Jerome H. Neyrey are major representatives of this method based on the sociology of knowledge—all reality is socially constructed and continued. Their investigations offer observations about social life and present a view of a micro-society in which a particular sect and its leader emerge.[54]

[52]L. Keck, "Toward the Renewal of New Testament Christology" *NTS* 32 (1986) 362–77, esp. 369–70.

[53]In addition to an early contribution of R. E. Brown *(The Community of the Beloved Disciple* [New York: Paulist, 1979]) see also J. Neyrey, *Christ Is Community: Christologies of the New Testament* (Good News Studies 13; Wilmington: Glazier, 1985).

[54]W. Meeks, "The Man from Heaven in Johannine Sectarianism" *JBL* 91 (1972) 44–72; G. Theissen, *Sociology of Early Palestinian Christianity* (Philadelphia: Fortress, 1977); H. C. Kee, *Christian Origins in Sociological Perspective: Methods and Resources* (Philadelphia: Westminster, 1980) and his *The Community of the New Age: Studies in Mark's Gospel* (Macon: Mercer, 1983); J. Neyrey, *An Ideology of Revolt: John's Christology in Social-Science Perspective* (Philadelphia: Fortress, 1988).

In assessing the method, Dennis Duling remarked that it is probably impossible to list an absolute set of guidelines for pursuing the analysis. Since the text reveals both the individual intentions of an author and the social worlds in which the author and the text exist, an awareness of different levels of analysis is basic. Norms and values of the social worlds must be investigated simultaneously with appropriate cross-cultural comparisons. Social roles derived from the text may be illumined by using redaction criticism for individuals and groups, as well as literary analysis for their characterization in the text. In particular, it is important to establish both the role of the disciples and their correlation with Jesus' role. The value of the social-historical method depends on how effectively it can provide data about the society(ies) behind the Christology as well as the Christology itself.[55]

Another method considers how narrative theory and literary criticism of the Gospels reveal a "story" perspective of Jesus and the disciples. An initial series on individual Gospel stories has been published in the present decade.[56] In addition, current periodical literature indicates a growing interest in the narrative approach. In Johannine research, R. Alan Culpepper has contributed a major study which clearly articulates a shift from historical-critical to narrative-critical analysis. In his *Anatomy of the Fourth Gospel: A Study in Literary Design,* Culpepper wrestles with a basic question of the historical-critical method: How does one understand the "truth" of a biblical text in relation to "history"? The question is crucial for the academy and the Church since the separation of Gospel narrative and objective history has caused divisions among scholars and communities of believers as well. Culpepper is convinced that it is the answer to the question upon which "the future role of the gospel in the life of the church will depend. . . . When art and history, fiction and truth are again

---

[55]D. Duling, "Insights from Sociology for NT Christology" *SBL Seminar Papers* 24 (Atlanta: Scholars, 1985), 351–68.

[56]Werner H. Kelber, *Mark's Story of Jesus* (Philadelphia: Fortress, 1979); O. C. Edwards, Jr., *Luke's Story of Jesus* (Philadelphia: Fortress, 1981); Robert Kysar, *John's Story of Jesus* (Philadelphia: Fortress, 1984); Richard A. Edwards, *Matthew's Story of Jesus* (Philadelphia: Fortress, 1985).

reconciled, we will again be able to read the gospel as the author's original audience read it."[57]

What response does he offer to this significant question? He identifies the gospel as story and indicates how it can be true if it is not "history." His assertion that the Fourth Gospel "develops narration, themes, characterization, ironies, and symbolism with a great deal of internal consistency"[58] is superbly argued and provides an alternative for studying the text in its discontinuities, i.e., an attribution of various sources and settings. His mastery and application of theoretical models to the Fourth Gospel enables a reader to grasp many complex relationships. In particular, the characterizations of Jesus, the disciples, the narrator, and the implied reader provide the context for Christological insights because the content of the narrative is inseparable from its form. Consideration of the Gospel as story assists the exegete in a Christological study which is not limited to one title or theme.[59]

A Christology of the Johannine Son of Man

The survey and evaluation of Johannine scholarship indicated attention to the origin of the Son of man and how it was related to the Synoptic Gospels. The primary question, however, is how the sayings function in the Fourth Gospel. Some scholars classified the sayings as secondary while others considered them integral to the text. A third group was interested in what situation in the community prompted the use of the Son of man in naming Jesus.

In contrast to most scholars, Margaret Pamment denied a Christological function for the Son of man, identifying the term as "Jesus' representative humanity." At the opposite end of the continuum, Francis J. Moloney maintained that the term provided a necessary corrective to the prominent Son of God Christology.

[57]R . A. Culpepper, *Anatomy of the Fourth Gospel: A Study in Literary Design* (prbk. ed.; Philadelphia: Fortress, 1987) v. See and compare: M. Pamment, "Focus in the Fourth Gospel" *ExpT* 97 (1985) 71-75; J. A. du Rand, "The Characterization of Jesus as Depicted in the Narrative of the Fourth Gospel" *NeoT* 19 (1985) 18-36; Gail R. O'Day, *Revelation in the Fourth Gospel: Narrative Mode and Theological Claim* (Philadelphia: Fortress, 1986).

[58]Culpepper, ix.

[59]Larry Chouinard, "Gospel Christology: A Study of Methodology" *JSNT* 30 (1987) 21-37.

His dissertation predicated a Son of man Christology specified in the human figure of Jesus who had been sent to reveal God to humankind. The Son of man reveals the truth because of the incarnation. While Son of God and Son of man refer to Jesus as the revealer and the revelation, Moloney maintains an absolute distinction between the two titles. The Son of man describes the human Jesus, and the Son of God designates the pre-existent Logos. The absence of Son of man in the Book of Glory (except for 13:31) strengthens the possibility of his distinction. He also criticizes Ernst Kasemann's *The Testament of Jesus* for failing to distinguish between the function of the two titles for Jesus.[60]

In contrast to Moloney's perspective, W. R. G. Loader posits a central structure for Johannine Christology (3:31-36), its recurring motifs, and its relationship to other Christological clusters—Messianic stream and the Son of man.[61] In the central structure of 3:31-36, the emphasis is on revelation. Jesus is identified as the Son who is sent by the Father and returns to him. His mission is to reveal the Father by speaking about and doing what the Father has communicated to him. The Father has given everything into the Son's hands. God is identified as the Father whose primary relationship is with Jesus as the Son. The motifs of the structure and their characteristic terminology appear frequently throughout the Gospel.

The Son of man cluster includes the title and motifs of Jesus' hour, his rising from the dead, glorification, ascension, judgment, and "something greater." According to Loader, the cluster is not integrated within the central structure of Christology; rather, it explains how the structure is to be understood. The cluster interprets how the Son of man is glorified through the story of Jesus' death and its significance. In the Book of Signs, the cluster and the central structure have different understandings of and terminology for descent and ascent, judgment and glory. In the Book of Glory, the Son of man cluster expresses "something greater" than the central structure. In the Last Discourses, the "terminological differentiation" disappears as Jesus reflects on his completed revelatory task (as Son) and anticipates his glorification

---

[60]Moloney, 208-14. See esp., 211-13 for schema of titular differences.

[61]W. Loader, "The Central Structure of Johannine Christology" *NTS* 30 (1984) 188-216.

(a characteristic Son of man motif). By abandoning the Son of man terminology, however, there is an integration with the central structure: "When the Son returns to the Father . . . a second Paraclete comes. . . . He makes known the Son, what he said and did."[62]

Unlike Moloney, Loader acknowledges a positive relationship between the central structure (Son of God) and the cluster (Son of man). He notes modifications of the tradition within the cluster. The exaltation of the Son of man becomes his return. His functions of judge and giver of eternal life become the foundation for sending the Paraclete who continues the activity of Jesus. The modifications arise from the Evangelist's conviction that the Paraclete fosters an account of Jesus' ministry wherein the central structure is confirmed by the Son of man cluster.

The Christology of the Gospel proposes a functional unity of the Son with the Father whereby Jesus is both a human being and a heavenly being, the Son of God. His relationship to God, however, is not substantial but functional. What Jesus reveals is not dependent on his being but on his relationship to the Father and where he has been. The central structure and the Son of man cluster indicate a developing Christology. The structure emphasizes a revelation of glory while the cluster indicates that Jesus' glory is not earthly but heavenly.[63]

Interpretation of the Author

My interest in examining the function and significance of the Son of man in the Fourth Gospel for Christology involved several procedures. First, surveying Son of man scholarship in the Gospels indicated that Synoptic scholarship appears at an impasse while Johannine scholarship is currently focused on the function of Son of man sayings and has benefited from the multiple approaches to the sayings. Second, examining the function of the Son of man was based on an exploration of the Fourth Gospel as story. As the *dramatis personae* used different terms to name Jesus, so Jesus used different terms to identify himself. Third,

---

[62]Ibid., 200.

[63]Ibid., 201-3.

reviewing how contemporary scholarship develops New Testament Christologies pointed out the importance of relating rather than ranking the names for Jesus.

The results I obtained from following these procedures provided a fundamental basis for concluding that the Gospel as story approach provides a contribution to Johannine Christology. What characteristics are indigenous to the approach? Three closely related features constitute the horizon for interpretation: *Variety:* The narrator employs a consistent differentiation of names and activities to describe Jesus. The variety, in turn, is corroborated by a frequent spiral technique which utilizes expressions in earlier chapters for new possibilities in later chapters. The integrated use of variety and spiral technique offers an inclusive reading of the Gospel which is more persuasive than any particular divisions imposed upon it. In addition, the variety which surprises and the spirals which reassure the reader function as a subtle, open-ended invitation to participate in the story on numerous levels of engagement no matter what the particular existential situation of the reader may be. *Lack of Closure:* The Gospel as story cannot be exhausted in a few readings. Each encounter changes with the varied circumstances of the reader as well as the insights derived from previous encounters. *Possibilities of Additional Disclosures:* The intriguing magnet of the Gospel as story draws individuals *and* communities of believers to consider what else they may discover in different situations, e.g., change of membership, circumstances (crises or insights), and evaluation of earlier interpretations.

The *fluidity* of the implications which derive from an interpretation based on the Gospel as story reflects the narrator's perception of Jesus. In particular, it may underscore a tension that the narrator and others experience about Jesus' identity. The tension of experience is clearly modeled in the encounters of Jesus and the characters in the text. The multiple strands of tension present there allow the reader to hear and see the identity of Jesus by what he says and does as well as by what the disciples and nondisciples say and do in response to him.[64] The fluid images of Jesus and others invite close inspection and attention. As catalysts they

---

[64]Cf. Chouinard, 30–32.

focus the reader's attention on reviewing options about believing and commitment.[65]

What does the method reveal about the images and names of Jesus in the Fourth Gospel? Leander E. Keck suggested that one approach to resolve the dilemma of the "paleontology of Christological titles" was to regard them as metaphors.[66] Drawing on Paul Ricoeur's work in biblical hermeneutics, Keck declared that metaphor offers new possibilities because it "deliberately sets up a clash between two things we know separately but do not identify in ordinary speech. . . . Metaphors live by the disparity of what is identified."[67] We know the name "Jesus." We know the terms by which he is identified. When "Jesus" is linked with any of these terms, a new insight may be revealed because the power of the metaphor consists in equating A with B, thus combining two different entities in a creative tension of relationship. Regarding titles as metaphors, the reader is alerted to the paradox implicit in the text. Why is new meaning possible? Ricoeur argues persuasively:

> Metaphorical interpretation presupposes a literal interpretation which is destroyed. Metaphorical interpretation consists in transforming a self-defeating, sudden contradiction into a meaningful contradiction. It is this transformation which imposes on the word a sort of "twist." We are forced to give a new meaning to the word . . . as an answer to a certain inconsistency of the statement interpreted literally.[68]

By accepting the metaphorical use of Jesus' titles (Son, Son of man, I am, Word [*Logos*]) and extending it to the symbols of life (light, water, bread), more than a juxtaposition of words occurs. In affirming the metaphorical dimensions of the text, a synthesis is created. Utilizing Ricoeur's insights about "root metaphor" revealing a capacity for relationship and a predication of deter-

---

[65]For further development, see Howard C. Kee, "Christology and Ecclesiology: Titles of Christ and Models of Community." *Semeia* 30 (1984) 171–92.

[66]See L. Keck, "Jesus in New Testament Christology." *ABR* 28 (1980) 1–20.

[67]Ibid., 12.

[68]P. Ricoeur, "Biblical Hermeneutics." *Semeia* 4 (1975) 78.

mination, there is a new understanding about the most frequent naming of Jesus as Son and God as Father in the Fourth Gospel. Certainly there are discoveries about unique relationships in the predication of the metaphors. Each one is a radical declaration dependent upon the reader's belief about the integrity of the witness of the text and the accompanying role of personal experience. In particular, the narrator clarifies how Jesus is Son by creating a new metaphor, Jesus is the Son of man. Moreover, new relationships about God, Jesus, and the believer are specified when the two principal metaphors are considered as connected to one another and to the overarching metaphor of believer as disciple.

What happens when Christological metaphors are pursued in the Gospel as story? Ricoeur expresses the process and the effect of a *new creation:* "the strategy of metaphor is heuristic fiction for the sake of redescribing reality. With metaphor, we experience the metamorphosis of both language and reality."[69] In the Fourth Gospel, Jesus as the incarnate Logos is both Son and Son of man who is the definitive revelation of God as Father in a communion of life offered as the definitive light for the human condition.

---

[69]P. Ricoeur, "Metaphor and the Problem of Hermeneutics." *The Philosophy of Paul Ricoeur: An Anthology of His Work* (eds. C. E. Reagan and D. Stewart; Boston: Beacon, 1978) 133.

Conclusion

In examining the Johannine Son of man according to the method of Gospel as story, I focused on three questions derived from interaction with the text. First, what is the function and significance of the Son of man for Johannine Christology? The interpretation of the Son of man sayings as *one* level of interaction between Jesus and the other characters provided an opportunity to study not only other relationships in the plot but also climactic moments of the narrative. The recognition of the metaphorical possibilities of the titles and symbols attributed to Jesus fostered a disclosure of Jesus through what he said and did in the narrative. The process provided an alternative to a study limited to the Christological significance of the Son of man sayings. The result is a recognition of the integral connection of Son and Son of man as two metaphors which invite the reader to reconsider the importance of the images and names used to describe Jesus as well as what they reveal about him as the incarnate Logos. The approach offers a broader perspective wherein the entire Gospel is the horizon for an interpretation whose final determination is not limited to a solitary or single reading. Metaphor offers multiple insights in successive readings. The significance of the Son of man, then, is located within what is revealed about Jesus throughout the Fourth Gospel as well as what the reader discovers which may extend beyond the understanding of a first-century community.

Second, can the function and significance of the Johannine Son of man be a dialectic for the Synoptic contours of the discussion?

A survey of scholarship indicated that a narrow base of interpretation had led to an impasse. Each method was applied to small units of text. A broader base of different methods for the same units or larger ones was not considered useful. Since seminal studies of the Synoptic Gospels as story have already been published, other scholars may be willing to assume the task of exegeting Jesus' titles as metaphors to bring new vitality to the Christologies of the Synoptic Gospels.

Third, what does this study offer to persons involved in the pastoral situations of teaching and preaching, liturgy and prayer? While the language issue in the Church is broader and deeper than changing a title of Jesus (God and persons) from an exclusive to an inclusive term, nonetheless, scholars may gain some perspective by remembering how interpreters translate a biblical text from its original language to a contemporary one. One of three techniques is usually chosen for various parts of the text: transliteration, substitution, or translation. This study proposes that the Son of man is a good translation for contemporary pastoral situations. It invites an individual or community to encounter the Fourth Gospel through assiduous reading and reflection, attentive to the surprises which a recognition of Son of man as a metaphor for Jesus provides. All language assumes the power of indicating a new reality. The language of the Gospel, especially through its metaphors, can dance through traditions and preconceptions. It can present to the attentive reader a challenge to participate in something new—a creative and freer way of being and responding to the Jesus identified in the story and metaphors of the Gospel.

Suggestions for Additional Reading

Culpepper, R. Alan. *Anatomy of the Fourth Gospel: A Study in Literary Design.* Rev. Philadelphia: Fortress, 1987. An excellent synthesis and interpretation of the Gospel as story. Comprehensive bibliography.

Donahue, John R. "Recent Studies on the Origin of 'Son of Man' in the Gospels." *Catholic Biblical Quarterly 48* (1986) 484–98. (Festschrift for J. A. Fitzmyer) A synthesis of Fitzmyer-Vermes debate; the contemporary situation and areas for additional research and clarification.

Moloney, Francis J. "The Johannine Son of Man." *Biblical Theology Bulletin 6* (1976) 177–89. A summary of his 1975 dissertation.

Neyrey, Jerome H. *Christ is Community: The Christologies of the New Testament.* Good News Studies 13. Wilmington: Glazier, 1985. An introduction to a method for analyzing Christologies in the Gospels and Letters. Helpful schematic charts.

Pamment, Margaret. "Focus in the Fourth Gospel." *Expository Times* 97 (1985) 71–75. A brief outline of the story approach to the Fourth Gospel.

_____. "The Son of Man in the Fourth Gospel." *Journal of Theological Studies* 36 (1985) 56–66. A brief discussion of each Son of man saying in the gospel in light of the contributions of Francis J. Moloney and Barnabas Lindar.

Vermes, Geza. *Jesus the Jew.* Philadelphia: Fortress, 1973. A classic text for his early thinking on Jesus as the Son of man (pp. 160–91).

Walker, W. O. "The Son of Man: Some Recent Developments." *Catholic Biblical Quarterly* 45 (1983) 584–609. A survey of Synoptic Gospel research in the context of six propositions and suggestions for additional research.